Reformation
Fire

Reformation
Fire

Martin Luther

Catherine Mackenzie

CF4·K

10 9 8 7 6 5 4 3 2 1

Copyright © 2016 Catherine Mackenzie

Paperback ISBN: 978-1-78191-521-9

epub ISBN: 978-1-78191-881-4

mobi ISBN: 978-1-78191-882-1

Published by Christian Focus Publications,
Geanies House, Fearn, Tain, Ross-shire,
IV20 1TW, Scotland, U.K.
www.christianfocus.com; email: info@christianfocus.com

Cover design by Daniel van Straaten
Cover illustration by Jeff Anderson
Printed and bound by Nørhaven, Denmark
Map illustrated by Fred Apps
Other illustrations by Neil Reed

Scripture quotations are based on the King James Version of the Bible.

Author's note: This material is based on the life of Martin Luther. Depending on which sources you use, what books, what articles, you may read different accounts of when particular events happened in the life of Martin Luther. When I came across conflicting information in my research I reverted to the book, *Martin Luther: The Man Who Started the Reformation* (ISBN: 978-1-85792-261-5) by Thomas Lindsay, originally printed in 1900. It is from this account that I have taken the timeline of Luther's life.

Contents

The Summer Storm

A small, sturdy seven-year-old boy sat by a narrow window. His mother had opened the shutters to let the air circulate. Everything that day seemed to be humid and stifling. In the distance, there were mountains, forests and the threat of rain. It was the perfect conditions for a summer storm.

As the sky began to darken, Martin thought he heard rumbling in the distance. Nervously, he tried to dismiss this noise as only the local mines and smelters … the smoking, belching workplaces of the local men who dug metal and iron out of the soil. Those noises he was used to, he could ignore them – dismiss them even as normal, day to day sounds … but Martin knew that what he was hearing in the distance was nothing to do with the sweltering work his father did, rather it was the mysterious noise that came every July and August, along with the humidity.

Martin shivered. His nerves were beginning to get the better of him. He knew the storm was on its way. Mansfeld could very well be in the thick of it before long. Once the storm passed over the neighbouring valley, he would soon see the lightning before the thunder rolled.

Out of the window, Martin had a good view of the little mining town he called home. It had bright red roofs and wooden-framed buildings. In the distance, a sturdy fence surrounded the area. It was there as a protection because Martin lived in a country that had to be prepared to fight. Towns and villages must protect themselves against raiders and opposing states. The land Martin lived in was called Germany, but it wasn't what you would call a united Germany, with one leader and one government. Instead, it was made up of lots of areas, each one ruled by its own prince, with its own army. Germany could be a volatile place and each town and village did what it could to fortify itself against enemies, real or imagined. However, Martin wasn't sure whether a fence like theirs would give any protection against thunder and lightning.

Martin's mother said that he should pray when he felt afraid. But Martin wasn't sure exactly who he should pray to. The priests prayed to the Virgin Mary and the saints – and there were lots of them. But his mother and father prayed to God. Simple prayers in German – different to the prayers he heard from the monks and priests in the chapel. They only ever seemed to speak in Latin. Frantically, as the thunder drew nearer, young Martin Luther tried to pray to the Virgin, all the saints and God, at the same time.

Confused and frightened, he hoped that someone would listen and help.

The storm continued to approach. Martin tried to take his mind off things by sniffing the familiar scents wafting on the air – the metallic aroma of the copper and silver mines, the fresh, almost medicinal, perfume of the pine forests in the distance, the closer floral notes of poppies and apple blossom from a well-kept family garden.

However, none of that could take his mind off the coming storm. 'Any moment now,' he whispered to himself. South-western Saxony in the summer was well used to sudden thunderstorms, but Martin was not. There was something about a thunderstorm that would always put him on edge.

'Be brave,' he told himself out loud. But Martin was not brave, and could not be, in the face of thunder and lightning.

Suddenly, across the ink-dense sky a serpent-like streak of fire lit up everything in its path. Martin leapt up with a gasp. Just then, a gentle voice at his left-hand side brought him back to earth. 'You know what to expect on summer days like these, my darling.' Turning away from the window and the terror outside, Martin looked into the grave, honest face of his young mother. Her high cheekbones were a sign of good breeding, or so she said herself. The sweat that slicked across her skin, however, was the evidence of hard work. Her warm, full mouth was what Martin loved most, because even though she used that mouth to discipline her oldest son, it was also the same mouth that told him she loved him and that had, for as long as he could remember, kissed him goodnight before he fell asleep.

'Why is it, Martin,' she asked, 'that you are always so scared of these storms?'

Martin interrupted, '… my heart jumps out of its skin at the sights and the sounds …'

His mother laughed, in a good-natured way. She recognised a little of herself in the anxious, poetic eyes of her young son. They could both take a leap of imagination and in moments be somewhere beyond the forests, in a land or world that they had never been in before. Martin's imagination, however, wasn't always beneficial, particularly today, as it led him to worry unnecessarily about something that happened frequently in their Thuringian homeland.

Martin's mother gave her little boy a gentle squeeze. She pulled him onto her lap, fully aware that she would not be able to do this sort of thing for much longer. Young lads had to grow up quickly in Germany, whether they were bound for the mines, like most of the young boys in Mansfeld, or for an academic life, like Martin.

Frau Luther wanted that sort of life for her eldest son. 'His bright mind and thirst for knowledge set him apart from the other lads,' she thought. Her husband, Hans, had spent a life slogging away in the dusty, dirty mines, drilling and digging silver and copper from the unforgiving soil. They both wanted something better for Martin.

Another streak of lightning broke directly overhead. The thunder that followed caused Martin to cling closer to his mother. Kissing him gently on the forehead once again, she smiled, trying to reassure him.

'Don't worry, Martin. This will soon be just another summer memory. I will not tell your father what a baby you have been. Just think of the power in that lightning as it streaks across the sky. Think of the power of its Creator. Think of what our God can do with the weather, and what he might do with just one life, like yours.'

Martin wasn't sure what God could do with a scaredy-cat like him. But the next thunder clap and the next died down in their intensity, each one sounding further away than the last. Finally, it was a distant rumble, with no lightning to be seen.

'There. All back to normal,' Martin's mother declared, pushing the boy gently off her lap and setting him firmly on the floor. Taking a small bag from the cupboard, she filled it with two portions of bread and an apple. 'No doubt you'll be hungry before suppertime,' she declared. 'Your father will be hungry too. All you Luther men have big appetites.'

Martin's pale face started to draw back some colour as he pulled on a cap to keep the last of the rain off his head. The thought of a snack before supper made him feel a whole lot better as he waved his mother goodbye.

Turning the corner onto the main street, he found himself in one of the busiest mining towns of the whole district.

'And father is one of the busiest miners in Mansfeld,' Martin thought to himself. His mother had told him so, many times. Martin's mother was proud of Hans Luther, her husband. Martin and his younger brothers would gaze in awe at the strong shoulders, piercing eyes and dark complexion of their father. He had worked his fingers to the bone to better his life and the lives of his children. It was a dangerous job mining, working deep underground, where a shift in the rock or soil could bury a man alive. Financially, it was troublesome too as Martin's father was continuously in debt, never owning the mines he worked in, only leasing them. It meant that the family had to borrow money in order to make money and feed the family. But the young Luther lads didn't know about the ins and outs of the mining business just yet. The harder aspects of a life in copper were kept from them. However, Martin's mother always reminded the Luther boys of what a respected father they had.

After taking a short cut and finding a convenient rock to stand on, Martin gazed out towards the tall chimneys that belched and billowed smoke from the hillsides. Piles of refuse surrounded all the mines. Deep holes and gashes had been dug out of the soil wherever a seam of copper and silver had been found.

Munching on his apple and bread, Martin scanned the horizon for his father. All the miners looked the same from a distance, small but stocky, sturdy in stature, a rolling gait. However, every time, Martin could point out his father in a crowd.

This afternoon was no exception. Almost immediately, Martin spotted one man, with one particular set of shoulders that said, 'Hans Luther.'

Martin ran, while his father waved and as soon as Martin leapt, his father caught him mid-air and swung him from one side to the other, like a pendulum.

'There's my boy!' Hans Luther exclaimed, dropping him again to the ground. It was a brief moment of friendship between father and son. As soon as it was over, Hans became the stern father once more, and Martin, his dutiful son. But the moment was still precious, even though it was short lived.

Hans and Margarethe were indeed stern in their discipline. Margarethe would chastise her children with word and action and Hans had once whipped Martin for taking a nut when he wasn't supposed to. But on this afternoon all thoughts of punishment were gone as the two Luther 'men' made their way home.

The older Luther looked on with pride at the younger Luther, and the younger Luther looked up with admiration at the older. The older one could see a bright mind and an even brighter future for his son, and the younger could see the best and strongest man in Mansfeld, if not the world.

'Oh, Father. Mother packed food for you also,' Martin smiled, passing his father the apple and bread.

'Hmmm,' his father licked his lips after taking a large bite of the home-grown fruit. 'Crisp and sweet, just the way I like it.'

Martin nodded. 'Mother knew you would be hungry ...'

'Your mother's a good woman,' Hans spoke between mouthfuls. 'She knows my stomach almost as well as she knows my face.'

Martin ate his own apple and continued to chatter all the way home. His father could hardly believe how quickly the seven years had passed since Margarethe, his wife, had brought this young scrap into the world. As the clock had struck midnight on St. Martin's day, their oldest son had taken his first, rasping cry, not in Mansfeld, where they lived now, but in Eisleben.

Hans then gazed up at the shadow of the large castle above them. Every penny he earned came with the permission or blessing of that family.

That was why he wanted something better for Martin. He wanted his son to have his own life, not to have to bow and scrape to counts and aristocracy. 'He should be a professor or a lawyer,' he muttered to himself.

Martin overheard, and puzzled, asked his father, 'What's a lawyer?'

Hans sighed. 'Scruffy little scrap,' he said, while ruffling his young son's hair. 'Your mother's right. If you're going to be a lawyer – if you're going to be anything – you will need an education.'

Martin gazed in wonder at his father. If he said it and his mother said it, then it must be true.

Education, Education, Education

'We're home!' Martin hollered as he and his father swung through the knotted, old wooden door that led straight from the street into the warm, slightly smoky kitchen.

Margarethe Luther was stirring the stew with an enthusiastic vigour. She was anxious to get dinner ready for her hungry husband and family. 'Fetch some more pine branches from under the eaves, Martin. I'll have finished these ones by the morning.'

Martin ran outside while his father pulled off his working boots and sat down wearily in one of the kitchen chairs. 'Do you really need more kindling or do you want to discuss our son's much-needed education?'

Hans Luther had come in the kitchen door and read his wife's face like a scholar reads a book: she wanted to talk to him in private.

Margarethe tasted a bit of the stew and decided to add a bit more seasoning. 'It is much-needed, Hans,' his wife agreed. 'But do we have the funding for it?'

Hans didn't reply directly, but thought to himself. An anxious expression spread across his face as he gazed into the flames of the kitchen fire.

'I've counted what we have in the strongbox. We're going to have to save more, whatever we can.'

Margarethe nodded. Both husband and wife knew what was in that box, or more importantly, what wasn't in it. There were other children to save for. The younger boys didn't show the same academic promise, but they would still need something for the future – to set them up in a trade or business. Margarethe was also pregnant again – it could be another boy, but this time it could be a girl. And girls needed husbands, and husbands needed dowries. It was all beginning to mount up.

Hans repeated what they had both said at one time or another, 'Martin shows more than usual promise. He's bright. He needs an education.'

Hans reached out to hold his wife's hand, while she stirred the pot with the other. 'God will provide,' he whispered as young Martin stumbled back into the kitchen with more wood.

Martin had overheard the word 'education', and asked, 'Does that mean I'll be going to school with Gunther? He says the master beats the boys and that the boys steal your lunch.'

'Humph,' Martin's mother was not impressed. 'That Gunther is always telling tales. Take no notice of him. His mother only sends him to school to get five minutes' peace. He's certainly not the brightest of the bunch.'

'Now, Margarethe,' Hans warned his wife quietly. 'You know ...'

'I know,' she muttered under her breath. How many times did her husband have to warn her about 'expressing' her opinions about the neighbours? 'But really, have you seen what those children get up to?'

Hans shrugged his shoulders and sat down at the kitchen table while Margarethe gathered the children in. 'Does Gunther know his Ten Commandments, like our Martin? I don't think so. Why, just the other week, I caught him scoffing my peas in the garden. Martin knows not to steal because we've taught him, "Thou shalt not steal."'

'I also know the Lord's Prayer and the Creed,' Martin added. But a quick scowl from both his parents reminded the young lad that children weren't supposed to muscle their way into adult conversations.

'Let us give thanks,' Hans Luther said, firmly, as he bowed his head and gave thanks for the food. That was the end of all references to Gunther, for now.

But Martin still wondered about what his young friend had said to him about all the punishments you got at school. Mother said it wasn't true, but the scar on Gunther's hand said otherwise. Gunther had said he'd done nothing wrong – which probably wasn't true. He was always misbehaving. But a scar – that was pretty serious, even for such a naughty boy as Gunther.

Martin's mother was sure that Gunther's family kept the local priests far too busy. 'The amount of time they must have to spend in confession – it's amazing the priests can pray for themselves or even eat!'

Frau Luther had cooked a goodly portion of stew that night, so there was enough for an extra scraping on Martin's plate. He licked his lips as she spooned it on. As the family finished their meal, Martin started to think to himself about all the times he had seen his mother and father go to confession. Martin had not yet gone there and he wasn't exactly sure what it was all about. All he knew was that people went to confession in order to tell the priests what they had done wrong. If they didn't do that, they wouldn't be forgiven for their sins.

'I'd better be careful,' Martin thought to himself, 'I could have too many sins to be forgiven when I'm old enough to go to confession.'

Martin started to count up the bad things he had done already that week, but he only got half way through Monday before he realised he might not be able to count all his misdemeanours.

'The priests must be very good men. They probably do not sin at all,' Martin continued to think as he scraped his plate. 'Father says that God forgives our sin because he is merciful. Will God be merciful to me?' Martin wondered. 'If I'm too bad, perhaps the priests won't let me go to confession at all. Perhaps they'll kick me out?'

Young Martin had lots of thoughts and questions. Even though his parents tried to teach him the right thing, many mistakes were being taught in the churches during those days. So Martin was beginning to pick up some wrong thoughts and beliefs. The situation would only get worse as Martin grew older. He would meet many people during his young life. Some would teach him wisely and some would hardly teach him anything at all. Others would teach him lies. But Martin's mother and father would teach him from their heart and from what they knew of the Word of God. Neither of them, however, would realise that one day God would use Martin to change the church and to teach the church in an amazing way.

At the end of the evening, with the supper things cleared away, Martin was allowed the honour of sitting with his parents by the fire. The younger boys were tucked up in bed. As his mother sewed, his father took his eldest son to one side, 'Martin, you will, I am sure, get on well with your education. I know you love learning. Your mother and I have taught you as well as we can. We have brought you up to trust in God, which is the greatest thing any person can learn. Not only that, you've had opportunities that other young lads have not had. Have you never wondered why I invited all these professors and preachers to visit our home? And why you were allowed to sit in and listen to the conversations?'

'Why, Martin, your father is right,' Margarethe added. 'It was for your benefit. Listening to these intelligent and godly men was good for your mind and your soul.'

Hans stretched his legs out, getting his toes as close to the fire as he could without getting his socks singed. 'Any learning that you have from now on must accomplish the same.'

After tucking him into bed and giving young Martin his usual kiss goodnight, his mother came back down the stairs to spend a few more moments in her husband's company.

'Here at this hearth we have taught our son the truth of God, but I am concerned. We need to be careful about this education,' Hans admitted.

'Why, husband?' Margarethe enquired. Surely education was what they had been planning for their son: a better life for Martin than the one they had had.

'So many schools and colleges these days do not teach what will bring a young man closer to God!' Hans exclaimed. 'Rather, they teach those monastic myths that I despise so heartily. Far too many monks and priests teach in the universities. God save Martin from those religious hypocrites! If God will only make Martin into a useful servant for him, I will rejoice. Come, wife,' Hans sighed, 'let us leave our troubles by the fire and with God's will, we shall find sleep before too long.'

The following days saw Martin's mother visiting the strongbox on more than one occasion. Firstly, Martin noticed that she took out some coins when the pedlar came knocking on their door. He had several tunics for sale. His mother spent some time studying the quality of the cloth and stitching. Holding up one against Martin's small frame, she decided to plunk down some hard-earned money on a dark green one. 'It's well made, and a good colour,' she commented.

Martin wasn't sure. 'Isn't it a bit big, Mother?' he asked.

'Nonsense, you will grow into it. What's the point of buying something that will be too small for you, come winter? There,' she said to the peddler. 'This is my final offer; take it or leave it.'

The pedlar was content to take it. Frau Luther drove a hard bargain, but it was a fair offer all the same.

Two days later, Margarethe came back into the house to dig out the strongbox once more.

'Gunther's mother is selling his slate and satchel. He won't be going to school with you next term. He's joining his father at the mines. And about time too. It's only hard work that will keep that one out of mischief for sure.'

Martin wondered whether he might prefer going to the mines with his father, rather than going to school. But he didn't think like that for long. He knew that he wanted to learn. Going to school was too good an opportunity to pass up on.

And as the summer heat began to pass and the thunderstorms became less frequent, the first day of the new term came closer.

With just a few days to go, Margarethe Luther had only one more problem to solve. 'Hans,' she asked her husband one evening. 'Martin is never going to manage that long trek to the schoolhouse. He was tired out this afternoon after we gathered in the firewood. The schoolhouse is further than the forest. What should we do?'

'That's already sorted. I've asked young Nicholas Oemler to help. He's big enough and strong enough to carry two Martins. So when your little boy gets tired, Nicholas will just swing him up on his shoulders and carry him the rest of the way.'

Margarethe smiled. Yes, Nicholas Oemler was a good choice. The sort of conscientious young man a mother could trust. Another thing she could tick off her list.

When the morning finally arrived, Martin pulled on his new tunic, tucked his slate inside his nearly new satchel and smiled excitedly as his mother stuffed in another apple.

Her instructions came quick and fast, about keeping his tunic clean and not eating his lunch before he got to school. Hans put his hand on his wife's shoulder with a gentle admonishment, 'Let the lad go. He'll be back before you know it.'

And with that, they both waved goodbye to their first-born as he made his way to school with a crowd of other young students.

'If the head can plan and the hands can labour, my lad shall be spared the grinding toil I knew and shall enjoy the splendid advantages I missed. He will be a great man and a scholar.' Hans said this out loud as Martin disappeared out of sight, on his way to a new life of learning and study. Education was important. They owed it to their young son to get him the very best!

But still in the back of Hans Luther's mind, and in the heart of Martin's mother, rang a note of concern.

Hans worried about the fact that there was indeed more to life than being a scholar.

Margarethe worried that her young son would soon realise that yes, masters did beat young boys.

A Ship of Cardinals

Martin had been so excited the night before his first day at school, he had barely slept. Tossing and turning on his straw mattress beside his little brothers, he had tried not to worry about all the tales his pals had told him about the stern schoolmaster. Martin had tried not to think about the long, tiring walk. Some parts of the path to the school house were very steep. But as he dropped off to sleep, finally he took comfort in the fact that one of the big boys had been told to carry him if he got too tired.

In the end, it was only the steep stretch towards the end that Martin needed help with; the long climb before the schoolhouse tower was visible in the distance. Nicholas had noticed that Martin was tiring and slowing down quite a bit. He heaved the youngster onto his shoulders and picked up the pace. 'If we don't speed up, Martin, we will be late and if there is one thing the schoolmaster hates, it's tardiness. We must, at all times, be punctual. The master beats those who turn up late.'

Martin gulped. Gunther's tales had been true, then.

Nicholas then smiled at his young charge and laughed. 'Don't worry about it ... you'll get used to the master's stern ways, and you'll learn to be a good scholar. Being disciplined is just part of being a student, Martin. So I'll stop talking. I need to use my energy in order to catch up with the other boys. They're quite far ahead of us now.' Nicholas then took longer, faster strides and before too long they were walking with the other lads and not far from the schoolhouse door. Nicholas put Martin down so he could walk the last bit on his own. Martin was glad. He didn't want to look like a little boy being carried into school. And as they arrived in the yard, the bell in the tower began to ring. Martin was relieved not to be late on his first day. That would not have been a good start.

Once the tolling of the bell stopped, all the boys had gathered in a line from smallest to tallest and stood smart and to attention in front of the school door. All the games had been left, all the laughing ceased. The master stood in front of them. He expected excellent behaviour and he got it. His gaze was stern. His moustache was impeccably groomed. His eyes seemed to slice through skin, right into a student's mind. Or that's what young Martin thought, as he gazed up with a mixture of fear and awe. Martin could imagine the schoolmaster as having special powers to know exactly what you were thinking, or even what you might be thinking in a few moments' time.

Martin, being the youngest and the smallest, was right at the front of the line. Never having been to school before, when the master barked 'Enter,' he had to be poked in the ribs by his neighbour. It was time for all the boys to march in and take their places on the floor. Martin hurried up the steps into the classroom where there were no chairs or desks. The only desk was the master's, situated against the wall at the back of the room from where he could see everything that was going on. Martin sat as close to the warm stove as he could and eagerly unpacked his slate.

There were quite a few faces in the schoolroom that Martin did not know. Boys came from lots of other farms and villages. No girls attended, as they stayed at home with their mothers. Any education they received was in bread making, sewing or other household skills. If their mothers could read and write, they might learn from them, but it was only the boys who were taught in the school. Girls didn't get much in the way of education.

Martin's report of his first day was a bit confused. The only thing he was absolutely certain about was the fact that he had enjoyed his lunch, every last scrap and bite of it. Even the seeds, stalk and core of the apple had disappeared down his throat. 'I'm glad I listened to your instruction, Mother,' he said on his return home. 'I could have eaten my food several times before lunchtime. Even at the corner of our road, I felt hungry, but I withstood the temptation and enjoyed my food all the more when mealtime came.'

His mother smiled and decided to put some extra cheese in his satchel the following morning. 'We can spare it for a growing appetite like his.'

'Gunther's tales about beatings might be true,' Martin thought to himself as he went to bed that night, 'but at least nobody stole my lunch.'

However, before too long, Martin realised that Gunther had told the truth about the lunch thieves and the beatings.

One boy tried to grab his apple off him and then Martin felt the sting of the master's strap for himself. He was so sore on the journey home that Nicholas actually had to lift him onto his shoulders to carry him down the hill, which was unusual. Martin was usually so pleased to be going home that the return walk wasn't so much of a problem. However, the little boy's sobs kept getting louder and louder, and the sores on his hands kept weeping. Nicholas gently lifted him up with a big sigh. He was sorry for young Martin, but a bit annoyed too. 'I know it hurts, Martin, but everyone feels the edge of the master's strap sooner or later.'

'But it wasn't my fault,' Martin sniffed as he tried to justify himself.

'You didn't know the Latin declensions,' Nicholas pointed out.

'The master never taught them to me,' Martin spat out the words from between his teeth.

When his mother put salve on the red welts that burst out of her boys soft hands, she tutted to herself.

Martin wasn't sure why – perhaps she thought he hadn't studied well enough. Martin wondered about asking his mother if he could stay at home the next day, but when he did, she tutted again. He was sent back to school as usual the next morning. Martin shuffled back into the classroom and knuckled down to his lessons once more, not knowing that his mother's angry looks and annoyance had not been for him. Already she was calculating what their next step would be.

'I'm not sending him off with one of those wandering students,' she declared emphatically. 'You hear terrible stories of how they treat their young charges. We have to send him to a high school.'

Hans Luther looked at his wife, nodding in agreement. 'But there isn't a high school in Mansfeld,' he pointed out. 'I agree with you that Martin is ready for it, and the present school he's in is just not good enough. So what do you think we should do?'

Margarethe laid out her plan with one word, 'Magdeburg.'

The school there had a good reputation.

'You know they still beat boys at Magdeburg if they don't know their Latin?' Martin's father reminded his wife.

'Yes, but at least they'll teach them the Latin they're supposed to know before they do that!' Margarethe declared, with a scowl on her face.

So, before too long Martin was withdrawn from the small schoolroom at Mansfeld and made his first trip into the larger German world. It wasn't an easier school, and in the end not much better. The care certainly wasn't good enough. Several months later, Martin was back in Mansfeld, recovering from what had been a very bad dose of fever.

Margarethe Luther was more than annoyed: she was livid. 'Is it too much to ask that those so-called bright and intelligent men look after our young son? They should have fed him properly, then he wouldn't have fallen sick. Did they keep him warm? I don't think so!'

Hans Luther kept his tongue silent as his wife continued to verbally chastise all the professors of Magdeburg.

As soon as his parents had heard of his illness, they had fetched their boy home immediately. Martin was now being nourished with good home-made soups and stews. His mother kept an eagle eye on him, any change in colour or appetite duly noted and dealt with by potions and poultices from her medicine chest.

One morning, Martin felt considerably better, well enough, in fact, to have a conversation with his mother about a painting he had seen in the Magdeburg church.

'What was in this picture?' his mother asked, sitting on the edge of his bed.

'It was a ship, full of cardinals and bishops and other churchmen. The pope was there too, at the prow. There were no ordinary men on board – not even a king or a prince. The priests and monks took the oars and they were sailing the ship to heaven.'

A frown crossed the brow of Frau Luther's face, she didn't like the sound of this picture. Martin went on, 'All the ordinary men, those who weren't priests or monks, were all swimming in the water around the ship. Some were drowning.'

Margarethe took in a sharp breath. The look of fear and worry on her young son's face concerned her.

Martin continued, 'The monks were throwing ropes to the drowning men to save them, so they too could come to heaven.'

Margarethe sighed. 'What is it that your father has taught you about getting to heaven?'

Martin stopped and thought. When no answer came, his mother reminded him.

'Pardon comes from the …'

'Ah! I know,' Martin shouted out, 'Pardon comes from the free grace of God!'

'Correct,' Frau Luther, breathed deeply. 'At least my boy hasn't forgotten all the good we taught him!' she exclaimed, before going on to remind Martin about the truth he had been taught. 'Heaven is for those forgiven for their sins. They don't get there because of good works or because a monk throws them a silly old rope. God, in his mercy, pardons a sinner – freely and without cost. I cannot fathom what you learnt at Magdeburg! All you seem to have returned home with is superstitious stories and a little more Latin grammar.'

Resting her hand on Martin's forehead, she noted the drop in his fever, and how his eyes were brighter and more focussed than they had been. Her son was on the mend. 'We'll keep you at home for a few more weeks yet, but when the next term starts, it will be Eisenach for you!'

'You are sending me to another school?' Martin asked.

'Yes, I've relations there. You won't be living with them, but it will be better for you. If you fall ill again, they can help. You'll stay in the dormitory in the meantime.'

Martin didn't feel that sure about this plan, as he had heard things about the school in Eisenach.

'Don't they make the boys sing for their supper there?' he asked.

Margarethe nodded. 'The school doesn't always make enough food for the boys to eat so they have to, on occasion, beg for their food to stop their hunger. Your father and I will help all we can. Our finances aren't that great. So you probably will have to sing, along with these other boys, to get some of your food. But it's possible the situation may change soon. Your father might be made a magistrate one day. Things may get better. But, for now, we all have to tighten our belts. You do have a lovely singing voice, Martin. I'm sure that will help.'

Martin didn't feel quite so confident.

Singing for your Supper

Martin Luther's first experience of singing for bread wasn't that encouraging; two slammed doors and an old crone who threw some crusts at him.

Martin gnawed on one of the crusts as he crept into his cold, damp bed that night. He longed for his straw mattress at home, the one he shared with his two wriggling, jiggling little brothers. Even though they kicked him in the shins, through the night, at least they were warm.

At other times during his stay there, Martin sang in the choir at St. George's church. Music played quite an important part in his life at school. But one evening, as he stood outside a comfortable looking town house, music turned his life in a different direction. His voice attracted the attention of the lady of the house.

'A little bread for the love of God,' Martin sang as she opened the door to her home.

Taking him into her kitchen, she fed him with soup and stew – nourishment he hadn't had since he had left Mansfeld.

'You cook almost as good as my mother!' Martin exclaimed, in-between a spoon of soup and a chunk of bread.

'Why, that is a compliment from such a sturdy young lad as yourself,' Frau Cotta declared. She could see that this young boy was hungry and that Martin was in need of care and a few square meals.

Eventually, she persuaded her husband to allow Martin Luther to stay as a guest-lodger in their home.

And it was there that Martin stayed until his high school days were over. It was just a few years after the young boy had started his lessons in Mansfeld, that he was now leaving Eisenach – taller, a little bit broader of shoulder, and with a much better education. Hans Luther was glad to hear his son's positive report on his return. The young man and the older man sat down at the open fire to share their news.

'The Cottas were so good to me, Father,' Martin smiled at the memory. 'It was as if I had another home. Their love for one another reminded me so much of you and Mother. Frau Cotta said to me that there is nothing more lovely than the love of a godly husband for a godly wife.'

Hans was delighted to know that Martin had met such a couple, with such common sense. Some of what he'd heard of Eisenach had been disturbing. There was certainly too much emphasis on monastic practices and the worship of the saints. But the Cottas sounded as though they were godly people.

Martin continued to tell his father about all the other things he had enjoyed at the new school.

'I learnt to play the flute at Eisenach. I will play it for you later, if you like.'

'Do that, son, after your mother has finished her tasks. At least that will be one thing you learnt that will give us joy. Hearing you recite Latin, however ...'

Martin laughed at the idea of calling out his Latin declensions for his parents. But the reference to Latin made Martin remember the wonderful teacher he had had in Eisenach.

'My master at St. George's was a distinguished gentleman.'

'A gentle-man, was he?' Hans smiled. 'You mean he was gentle with the strap?'

Martin laughed again. 'There was certainly less need for it, shall we say. And he would bow to the whole class every morning — as if we were noblemen ourselves — though some of us had more of the appearance of peasants than gentry.'

Hans looked puzzled. He had not heard of this kind of treatment before. Martin went on to explain.

'He would act so because he believed "future burgomasters, chancellors, doctors and magistrates are among those boys."'

'Hmm,' Hans nodded thoughtfully. 'He'll be right. Certainly, Martin, you'll have the pick of all those careers.'

Martin nodded, though he wasn't sure which one he should choose. How could he please God in his career if he happened to choose wrongly, selfishly or greedily? Which of these occupations would please God most? How could his work bring him peace with God – the peace he craved most of all?

As he went to bed that night, Martin worried that he was on the wrong path. He was concerned. Lots of the monasteries and convents in Eisenach had been devoted to a particular saint called St. Elizabeth. 'Perhaps I should pray to her,' Martin thought anxiously. 'She is an important saint, after all, and I remember the time I saw her image lit up in the church.'

Martin let his mind wander back to that sunlit evening when he had entered through the large wooden doors to see the last rays of the sun hit against St. Elizabeth's stained glass window. Her image had looked as though it was on fire. The sun picked out the engravings of all her good works. She was renowned for giving up her family life and children in order to become a saint. Martin had felt as though the woman was coming to life in the glass window. Her magnificent saintliness shone out in utter brilliance. The memory burned in his mind once again.

'St. Elizabeth, help me,' he whispered as he knelt by the side of the bed. Several hours later, Martin struggled back underneath his blanket, unsure if any of his words had been heard at all. 'Did St. Elizabeth hear my prayer?' he asked himself. 'I'm not sure if even a mouse heard what I had to say.'

Martin would have been better sharing his concerns with the living, godly woman who, as he fell back to sleep, was now waking from her slumbers in the room next to him. She went down the stairs to sweep the hearth, make the breakfast and care for the household's needs. She didn't abandon home and family for so-called saintliness. She served her family and God because she was a real saint – one who slogged, one who struggled and one who believed in the true God. She couldn't read Latin, she had never had much of an education, but she would have been a better guide than a dead image, painted on a window, unable to say anything at all.

For all his wonderful education, the sad fact was that the honest peasant faith that Martin had been brought up with was being watered away by the influences of the mystic superstitions, rife amongst monks, and Catholic relics. Martin's family had brought him up in a truthful, pious faith, pure and simple. There wasn't a lot of knowledge there. They didn't have access to a Bible, but what they did know, they had taught their children. Yes, they made mistakes, but both parents were well aware of the dangers of false teachings. However, despite his godly parents, there was something in Martin's mind and heart that was drawing him away from the truth of the Bible.

As Martin got ready to head off to university at Erfurt, Hans and Margarethe felt that their plans were now really bearing fruit. Financially, they were better off and could pay for Martin's university education. They also had enough money set aside to help their other sons begin homes of their own. Their daughters too were provided for. One of Martin's sisters was courting that young man, Nicholas Oemler, who had heaved young Martin onto his shoulders on the way to school.

Martin couldn't believe it when he heard, 'The young man who carried me on my way to school is now going to carry off my sister!'

Frau Luther smiled at her son's wit. Things seemed to be coming together well. 'Yes, Martin, the Lord has been good to us. Not only are we able to send you to university, and provide help for your siblings as they start out in life, but this time we'll be able to provide for your food and accommodation at university. No more singing in the streets for you, or relying on the charity of others. You'll be able to devote all your time to your studies. You know what they say: anyone who wants to study well must go to Erfurt.'

Martin studied very well at university and got his Bachelor's degree in 1502, and shortly after, in 1505, he gained his Master's. However, there was more to Martin Luther's years in Erfurt. During his time there, he struggled in a great battle – not a battle with swords and pikes – but a battle for his soul.

It had probably begun when he was quite young, perhaps when he had seen the painting in the chapel and had witnessed so many people praying to St. Elizabeth. However, now the battle was beginning in earnest.

Things happened during his stay in Erfurt that deeply affected him. A grave illness had him at death's door. A good friend died. Many things made him question how he was ever going to get to heaven. It tortured his mind and soul with very little, if any, relief.

His mother and father had no idea what was going on. They just felt relieved that their eldest son was at university. It was exactly what they had planned for their boy from his earliest days, when he had begun to show such promise. Martin had come second out of seventeen students in his exams, so it seemed to Hans and Margarethe that their dreams had indeed come true.

But again, Martin's heart was being pulled away from the truth by false religion. His university life was a double life. He spent hours in study and books, dressed in his academic robes, preparing for a life as a lawyer. Yet he was also tangled in a net of religious traditions and rituals that involved prayers for the dead and listening to endless eulogies for the Virgin Mary. On the one hand, Martin wanted to honour his parents' hopes and dreams, but on the other, he felt that he would give everything up if only he could be at peace with God. The more he thought about it, the more he wondered about that picture. It was only monks and priests on board the ship – it was only the religious men who were on their way to heaven. Martin had no idea that all those years ago in Magdeburg, he had seen a lie created with parchments and paint – and that lie had infected his very soul.

Perhaps if Martin had been able to study the Bible more, he would have been brought to realise the truth. But even though Martin studied theology and church law, God's Word was not a book he was that familiar with. The Bible was not a title that people had much access to. Most people couldn't read Latin and the Bible wasn't published in German. When Martin read books he was reading books about the Law. 'But will the law help me have peace with God?' he asked himself.

Questions like this plagued Martin. His heart was greatly burdened. Martin Luther was being assaulted spiritually.

After his graduation, Martin made a brief visit home to enjoy the pride of his parents and some good home cooking. Hans and Margarethe smiled, overjoyed that their young lad had fulfilled his potential. But as they waved him goodbye on his return journey to Erfurt, they weren't to know that their plans were about to be blown to the four winds.

As the nineteen-year-old Martin turned round on his fine-looking horse for a last goodbye wave, a rumble in the distance made Margarethe look beyond the forests. A dark sky in the distance promised a storm.

'I hope it doesn't hit before he gets back.'

'He's not a child, Margarethe,' Hans scolded, as they made their way back into the house.

'No, but he is still Martin, and that's still a thunderstorm,' she muttered, 'if I'm not mistaken.'

Another Thunderstorm

Martin felt the familiar clammy sweat on his skin. He had ridden several miles from Mansfeld and the air had the feel of thunder, but he urged his mount on, ignoring the knot of fear in his stomach. A few moments later, the sky became blacker than usual, large drops of rain began to fall. A storm was approaching. 'If I pick up the pace,' Martin decided, 'I may be able to stay ahead of it. Keep going, Martin,' he urged himself. Pressing his thighs into the flanks of his horse, the animal broke from a slow trot to a canter.

But no matter how fast they rode or how far the distance they covered, the storm still followed. Martin looked at the sky and couldn't help but compare it to how he had been feeling these last few months. Everything had been so dark and gloomy since his best friend had been laid in a cold grave. There was a question over the young man's death. Martin even wondered if he had indeed been murdered, although that wasn't certain. 'Where is my friend now?' Martin asked himself. He had no comfort for his companion in eternity. Martin also feared for his own soul. He often felt that he was drowning, like the men in the picture. He longed to be with the monks and priests safe in that ship, heading for heaven. But nothing these days brought peace or joy to his heart.

'I know my soul is in real danger,' he muttered as he looked up again at the ever-darkening sky. 'I can see no salvation, no heaven, only hell. The death of my friend has just made this feeling worse than before. I have a certain knowledge that death will not bring relief, just more eternal suffering.'

The storm in his own heart was soon to be echoed in the storm that chased him across the Thuringian sky.

Lightning cut a gash across the heavens and the thunder came moments later. Martin knew that the threat was very real now. Another bolt of lightning hit a tree nearby. As the sparks flew, Martin's horse screamed, rearing up on its hind legs, eyes bulging, breath hot and Martin struggled to keep it under control. The storm was on every side, surrounding him. He was afraid – not just of death, but of what lay beyond it: eternity, the fear of hell and never having access to heaven. Martin was as panicked as the horse. With a strong tug on the reins, the beast pulled itself out of Martin's grasp and vanished over the horizon. In his terror, Martin called out to yet another dead saint, 'Help me, St. Anne, and I will become a monk!'

It might seem that Martin blurted out something in the spur of the moment. It certainly was rash, but Martin's thoughts about death and hell had been plaguing him for some time. He had been wondering what he should do to gain eternal life. Unfortunately, he had not had godly guidance. Martin had been influenced by false doctrines and heresies, which was why, in this moment of trial, he turned towards a dead saint instead of the living God.

Martin stood shivering through the rest of the storm. When it had past, he continued the rest of the route to Eisenach on foot, where, two weeks later, Martin became a monk, to the astonishment of professors, friends and family alike.

In fact, Martin was probably in the monastery before his parents had even heard of his decision.

Here was a young, promising law student throwing himself away into a monastic life.

In the days before he entered the monastery, many quizzed him about his motives.

'What made you do it?' a friend asked. Martin handed him one of the books he would no longer need as a monk and replied, 'I was afraid.' He didn't have any other explanation.

'What are the professors going to say?' the friend asked. 'Forget that! What are your parents going to say?'

Martin groaned. He was moments away from closing himself inside a monastery and he could only guess at what his parents would say.

'You haven't told them?' his friend asked, incredulously.

'I wrote a letter. If they don't know, they will soon.'

Martin's friend shook his head. Both young men knew what a bitter disappointment this would be to Hans and Margarethe.

Martin muttered, 'What I am about to do will save my soul. It is better that my parents are kept out of this decision. I can't risk them persuading me against it.'

What Martin didn't realise was that his soul was in danger, and that rescue was only available from Jesus Christ. However, Christ was able to save him inside or outside of cloisters. Martin was being led away from the real truth and the real Christ. Instead of being led into a life of peace with God, the next few years would be a life of despair and spiritual imprisonment.

Martin Luther entered the Augustinian monastery on the 17th of July, 1505. The last words he said to his university friends and professors before he went through the cloister gates were, 'Today you see me; after this you will see me no more.'

As Martin's parents opened the letter to read their son's heartbreaking news, both wondered what they had done wrong and how all their plans had come to nothing in such a bewildering way. The box that came with the letter contained Martin's clothes, which he no longer required for his life as a monk, and the ring he had been given on his graduation.

Martin's father angrily replied to Martin's letter as his wife sat woefully at the window seat as yet another thunderstorm rolled over the hillside.

'Why, Lord God? Why?'

This was not what she had prayed for … a son throwing away his gifts for a life of false friars and fake faith. She knew enough of the monastic life to know its shallowness. The vow that Martin would now take would mean he would no longer be her son. His heart and hands would be for popes and not the parents who had loved him and cared for him all his life.

'Their hypocrisy!' The words came spitting out of Hans's mouth. 'Their false piety! They pretend to follow Christ but they ignore Scripture.'

Margarethe sighed, 'One of the first commandments we taught Martin was, "Honour thy father and thy mother" (Exodus 20:12). Why, then, has he abandoned this commandment and the many other truths we taught him, to live a life as a monk?'

Silently, she bowed her head and prayed, 'Lord, do you yet have a plan for our son?'

Peering once more out the window, she caught another glimpse of lightning. The summer storm passed over the mountains.

'All those plans we had for his education, university, the law …' She felt slightly foolish now, as well as bitterly disappointed. 'The Lord's plans were not our plans. Father, forgive me.'

Then she stood up and went once again to the fire and the pot. Stirring the ash, the flames lit up again. There was food to cook and a home to warm. Storms came and storms went, and it was the same in family life as it was in the natural world. As this recent storm bypassed Mansfeld, her eldest son was walking straight into a storm of his own making.

Miles away, her eldest son stood in front of the prior, about to change his life, as he thought, for ever.

'What seekest thou, my son?' the Augustinian prior asked earnestly.

Martin replied, as thousands had done before him, 'I seek the mercy of God and your fellowship.'

With that, he was accepted as a novice to the order of the Augustinian monks. His initiation would take one year, where he would learn all the details and practicalities of being a monk.

This year was full of rules that governed every moment of his life. Several hours in the day were devoted to hearing chants and reciting prayers.

Martin had to learn how to do everything just so. Many days, the men in the monastery, for it was just men who lived there, had to fast. That meant going all day without food and spending even more time than usual in prayer. There were so many rules to obey. You had to stand a certain way, sit this way or kneel like that. You had to wear a monk's habit and have your hair cut in a tonsure, which involved having a bald circle on the top. After a year of submitting himself to all these rules and practices, Martin was ready to become a monk.

The church was full of Martin's friends and professors from the university. Townspeople from Erfurt were there too, but none of Martin's family. Martin wasn't surprised, but it was still disappointing. It had been so long since he had seen his parents. The angry letter from his father had been their last communication. 'Who knows when we will see each other again?' Martin wondered.

But now came the time for Martin to make his vows. He knelt before the prior and uttered the following words: 'I, Brother Martin, do make profession and promise obedience to Almighty God, unto Mary the Virgin, and unto thee, my brother, prior of this cloister, in the name and stead of the General Prior of the Eremites of St. Augustine, until death.'

Over the black hood and robe of the order of the Augustines, a long, white scapulary, or scarf, was laid. A lighted taper was placed in Martin's hands, prayers were said and songs sang as Martin was led up the altar steps.

He was welcomed into the order by the other brothers, as he slowly marched behind a screen, no longer part of the outside world, but a monk.

'What a waste,' muttered one of Martin's friends. 'If I had half of his intelligence, I tell you, I'd be out there making a name for myself. Yet Luther has now disappeared into a life of prayers and penance.'

Another young man agreed, 'He could have been one of the great men of the university.'

An old professor sighed. He'd seen other men like Martin make exactly the same decision and it bewildered him. 'What makes them do it?' he asked.

'They believe that the best way to serve Christ is to give up home and family,' muttered another onlooker.

'Hmm, the vow of celibacy, never to marry, holds no attraction to me,' exclaimed another.

'It's more than that,' a young man added. 'They give up all worldly goods.'

'Almost all,' one of the students added. 'I hear Martin still has his Virgil.'

The old professor laughed. 'How like Luther! The one personal possession he takes into the monastery is a book. Monk Martin's guilty secret is a volume of poetry. Maybe there's hope for him yet.'

'I doubt it,' another younger professor butted in. 'The monastery has its claws in Martin now. Latin and law books could not satisfy him. The monks simply stepped into the breach with promises of salvation.'

'Martin was always overly conscious of his sin, in my opinion,' a rather pompous student declared. 'He'll make a very serious job of being an extremely virtuous monk, I'm sure. It's the perfect sort of life for him … top of the class, every professor's favourite.'

'Watch out, you're beginning to sound jealous,' another student pointed out.

'Jealous? Me? Never! I'm certainly not jealous of a monk in a scapulary, with a shaved head and a life hidden away in a monastery. Let him enjoy that life, if he can.'

With that, Martin's friends and professors disappeared to their own lives and studies. They might think of Luther occasionally in the future, but not often, at least not until another incident brought him back to their attention – and the world's.

Fear, Faith and Forgiveness

Luther now disappeared into the life of prayer and fasting, vows and observances that was the life of a Roman Catholic monk. The rather pompous student was right – Martin was taking his job of being a monk very seriously – perhaps too seriously.

You see, the whole problem with the Roman Catholic Church at that time was that it had drifted away from the truth of the Bible. It had been going on for years. And nobody had been able to stop it. There were still people in the church who trusted in God, who sought forgiveness for their sins from their Creator, rather than their priest. Some still believed that the only way to be forgiven was through the mercy of God, through Christ's death on the cross. However, false beliefs had crept into the church too. Many people, for instance, went to confession, believing that it was only the priest that could ensure God would forgive them. They would come to a cathedral or church building and kneel before the priest in private, telling him all the sins they had committed since their last confession. The priest then would 'absolve' them of their sins. He would pray for them and instruct them perhaps to pay a penance in order to be forgiven. This could mean doing good deeds, or reciting certain prayers. However, the Bible does not tell us that we need to go to anyone to be forgiven – only Christ. We only need to approach God in the name of Jesus Christ to be saved. The Bible, in Isaiah 64:6, tells us quite clearly that our good works cannot save us, they are just like filthy rags – of no real use to anyone.

During Martin Luther's lifetime, many people believed that you should pray to the Virgin Mary and the saints for forgiveness. Cathedrals said that they had the finger of St. Peter, or a piece of the cross Jesus died on. People foolishly believed them. They would make special visits to see these relics, as they were called. Once they arrived, they would pray in front of these old bones in order to get special benefits. But again, the Bible tells us that we are to pray to God directly, that we don't need to pray to other people, like saints, in order for God to listen to us. The Bible tells us that God is the hearer and answerer of prayer. God hears sinners. As well as that, if you believe that Jesus alone is the Saviour of sinners, that makes you – an ordinary person – a saint! Saints are forgiven sinners. It's God's love and forgiveness that makes them so, not their good works. It is God who cleanses them from sin, not their own acts.

But this was what people in Martin Luther's time were getting rather confused about. Martin was confused about it too. He thought that going to the monastery would save him, that keeping his vows would get him to heaven, that working very hard at being a monk would make him holy and please God. But it simply wasn't true.

Martin had pinned all his hope on being like one of the monks in the painting. He believed that was the only way to heaven. He was sorely mistaken.

How disappointed and upset his parents would have been if they had seen all that Martin did in order to 'please God'. They had taught him about God's mercy. They didn't believe that vows and even good works could save someone from hell – only God could do that.

Martin, however, spent hours without food, praying in his bare little cell – a tiny room where monks would pray and sleep. In fact, Martin sometimes only prayed there. He often forced himself to do without sleep – another foolish act that he felt would please God and save him from eternal suffering. Martin would just spend hours and nights in prayer in order to punish himself for his sin. He thought that if he treated his body in this harsh way, he wouldn't want to sin so much.

Martin's actions became so extreme that they even started worrying the other monks.

One day, there was a knock on the prior's door.

'Come in, Brother Justin,' the prior called out. 'How can I help you?'

Prior Staupitz could see on the face of the other monk that there was a problem.

'It's Brother Martin,' the man replied. 'We've just found him collapsed on the floor of his cell. It was only because he was missed at the service that we thought we'd better check on him, to see what was wrong.'

'Have you taken him to the infirmary? Our healers should be able to help.'

The monk nodded his head, but still looked a bit concerned.

'Is there something more?' Staupitz asked.

'Well,' Brother Justin shuffled on his feet as he worked out what he should say, 'Apparently, Brother Martin has been in prayer and fasting for over three days. There are scars on his back from where he has been whipping himself.'

Staupitz sighed and shook his head. 'If there is any more news about our brother, keep me informed.'

The monk nodded and retreated from the room. Staupitz drummed his fingers on the wooden desk, an ink well and a scroll – the only things that were within his reach. An icon on the wall was lit up by the light coming through from the only window in the room. Staupitz knew what it was like to live a simple monastic life, but young men like Martin concerned him. They were obsessed about so many things, but missed out on what really mattered.

Though Staupitz followed many of the false teachings of the church at that time, he hated some of the extremes that people went to in order to be at peace with God. He knew it seldom brought real comfort. 'I'll visit our brother in his sick bed,' Staupitz said to himself. 'Some careful guidance and advice may be all he needs.'

Later on, Staupitz gently urged Martin to spend more time reading the Bible. 'I insist that every monk who is able, must study theology. For that reason, there is a Latin Bible in every convent.'

Martin gingerly raised himself up in his bed. This was a new sort of advice. Staupitz held the patient's hand.

'Study God's Word,' he urged. 'Spend your time there rather than in fasting … and scourging.' He said that last word with a stern tone to his voice.

Martin nodded, but was slightly confused. Didn't this wise monk want him to subject his sinful flesh to godly punishment? Didn't he realise how sinful Martin was? Staupitz saw his confusion and realised its source.

'Martin, I've seen how much time you spend in the confessional. Were you to spend half that time in reading God's Word, the brothers wouldn't have found you near death in your cell this morning! In fact, what I have to say to you is this: stay away from the confessional until you have some actual sins to confess!'

With that, the prior gathered his robes together and walked briskly out of the room. As he exited, he called back to the patient, 'I don't want to see you in this ward again, Brother! It's all gone too far in my opinion!'

Later that night, Martin's sighs and groans were echoing around the corridors. The elderly monk in charge of the infirmary knew that it was more than just aches and pains that bothered his patient.

Quietly, he approached Martin's bed to try and comfort him. 'Are you in pain, Brother Martin?' he asked.

Martin shook his head.

'Then what troubles you?' the gentle monk asked.

'My sin, my sin,' Martin trembled as he said the words.

The wise old monk simply said, 'Repeat the Creed.'

Now the Creed is a selection of words that had been put together by the church many years before. It summed up the central beliefs of the church and had been taken from Scripture. It had a particular name, *The Apostles' Creed.*

I believe in God the Father Almighty Maker of Heaven and earth, and in Jesus Christ, His only Son, our Lord; Who was conceived by the Holy Ghost, born of the Virgin Mary; Suffered under Pontius Pilate; was crucified, dead and buried; He descended into hell; The third day he rose again from the dead; He ascended into heaven, and sits at the right hand of God the Father Almighty;

From thence he shall come to judge the living and the dead.

I believe in the Holy Ghost; the holy Catholic church; the communion of saints; the forgiveness of sins; the resurrection of the body; and the life everlasting.

As Martin repeated these familiar words, ones that he had learnt at his mother's knee, the old monk stopped him just before the end, just as he was saying the words 'the forgiveness of sins'. He asked Martin, 'Do you believe that?'

'Believe what?'

'Do you believe in the forgiveness of sins? Repeat it again, but add in the word 'my'. I believe in the forgiveness of 'my' sins.'

Martin thought about the words as he muttered them quietly to himself. Did he believe that? He couldn't say for sure.

The monk left him to his thoughts with the words, 'God has promised us pardon.'

It gave him a few moments of comfort, but just that. Martin was soon over-thinking things again and dwelling on himself rather than on God.

'To be pardoned, I have to be sorry for my sin, I must confess and do penance, but am I sorry enough? Is my confession enough? Have I done enough? I have sinned so much, I must have forgotten some sins, if not many. God is so holy, how can he forgive a sinner like me? How can I come to God and ask him to forgive me?'

Such troubled thoughts kept assaulting Luther in the hospital and out of it. Staupitz was very concerned, and others were too. Brother Martin was clearly in a spiritual struggle. The elderly monk who had cared for him in the hospital, brought his concerns to the prior.

'He seems to think that God is against him. He sees God as righteous and holy and himself as a sinner and unholy … and this is right … yet, as always, Martin takes everything to extremes.'

Staupitz nodded, his arms folded as he looked out the window of his room. 'How can we explain to Brother Martin that God is on the sinner's side? God's righteousness is for everyone who trusts in Christ. Send him to the Scripture again. This time, suggest that he makes a study of the Book of Romans.'

This was how Martin found himself once again – reading the red leather-bound Latin Bible that Staupitz had first told him about that day in the infirmary. He had read it before and had enjoyed discovering the story of Samuel. There had been something strangely comforting about the character of Hannah, a mother figure who reminded him of his own waiting at home in Mansfeld. However, this time, something in the Book of Romans lit up Martin's mind. There was warmth in his soul that hadn't been there before.

A few simple words caught his eye, 'The just shall live by faith' (Romans 1:17).

Straight away, Martin saw something new, felt something new, believed something new … new at least to him; it was, in fact, as old as time itself, and older.

Martin realised that it was God's righteousness, God's compassion; God's mercy that was needed, all that was needed to be saved. It was all about God's work and not about him.

Martin's sin, which had been bothering him for so long – from before he had entered the monastery – was now not separating him from God because God had washed it away. In exchange, Martin had been given Christ's righteousness, and as a result, Martin was in a deep peace with God. Everything he needed spiritually had been given to him by God – faith, forgiveness, even his repentance.

'Before, I used to fear and quake at the words, "God's righteousness". It would afflict me with terror more than a streak of lightning or a crash of thunder. But now these words fill me with a flame of love, a fire of joy … my darling, and comforting Word of God, a true door of paradise!'

Martin looked again at the words on the page before him – black ink, as black as his sin. And it was these words that had brought a cleansing to his soul.

'If I had known these words before, perhaps I wouldn't have felt the need to come to this monastery … for in one sense there certainly was no need for me to come here. But I'm still glad I came, for it is here that I have read God's Word and it is here that I have believed it.'

But God's Word wasn't finished with Martin Luther … there was still more he needed to know and believe and there was still much he needed to re-learn. The heresies of the church, at that time, were rife. Though there were wise old monks and gentle priors, there were still many church leaders living a godless, selfish, false life, and misteaching others to live the same.

The Devil's Delusion

One day, a letter was sent from the monastery to Mansfeld. Martin was going to be ordained as a priest and he would be taking his first Mass.

Hans Luther held it limply in his hand before saying to his wife, 'I'll go. You needn't come.'

Margarethe nodded. It wasn't something she wanted to witness. Becoming a priest was the point of no return for their son. She had hoped, up till now, that somehow Martin would change his mind and leave the monastery. Sometimes monks did that, though it was rather rare. But priests – that was different. She had never heard of a priest leaving his profession. Not once.

On the day of his first Mass, Martin's nerves got the better of him. Perhaps it was something to do with seeing his father again after all this time. Hans still had a dark scowl of disappointment on his face. Martin was desperate to prove to his family that he had made the right decision, but he blundered and spluttered his way through the ceremony and didn't really make that great an impression.

At the ordination dinner, he turned to his father and asked him to his face, 'Why are you so set against me?'

The whole table went quiet as the young priest continued with his accusation.

'You are still so unwilling to see me as a monk – I don't understand. This is such a peaceful and godly life.'

Hans Luther looked at his son, then at the professors, masters and monks that sat around him. Standing up amongst this crowd of learned men, the copper miner from Mansfeld spoke directly to the ones he believed had stolen his eldest child.

'Did you never hear that a son must obey his parents? The Holy Scriptures say a man should honour his father and mother. You argue about the beauties of the monastic life. You say, my son, that you have simply followed the divine call! God grant that it may not prove a delusion of the devil!'

With that, he handed over a gift to the convent of twenty gulden and left.

Martin now went into his life as a priest with the same energy and conviction that he had brought to his life as a monk. He never did anything by halves. Plenty of monks and priests did as little as they could get away with. Martin, however, did as much as he could … even more than he should.

His duties now included conducting services such as the Mass and taking confession. Though his thoughts on the Mass had changed a bit, his opinions on confession were now quite different to what the church thought.

As regards the Mass, he would always believe that the actual body and blood of Jesus were present in some way – but he did not believe that the Mass had any virtue on its own. Without faith in God and in his Word, it was worthless. When it came to confession, Martin still allowed people to come to him to confess their sins, but he didn't absolve them of their sins. Instead he guided them to God, who alone could forgive their sins. He told sinners to go to Christ rather than to their own works. So in the confessional he gave advice, helping others to see forgiveness was from God alone.

Martin began to prove himself as a competent individual, one who could be trusted. In the year 1508, Martin was asked to take on more responsibility.

The ruler of Saxony, or Elector Frederic as he was known, had just formed a university in Wittenberg. Staupitz and a man called Dr. Pollich were discussing the elector's plans. Both men were close advisors to the German ruler, were largely responsible for increasing the income for the university. That was one thing that universities always needed ... money.

The other thing they needed was good professors. The two men came up with a way of saving money by getting very good professors. How did they do that?

'Everything has been spent. All that is left must be kept for the professors' wages. I don't know what to do,' Pollich complained.

'I do,' declared Staupitz. 'You still need to fill the positions in theology and philosophy, yes?'

'Don't remind me! How are we going to get professors for those disciplines and pay them a decent salary?'

'Well, I have the perfect candidate for you, and you won't have to pay him anything.'

'Staupitz, don't tease me. Where are you going to get someone like that?'

'We'll ask Brother Martin, of course! We should use him and others like him. They're monks, so they don't need a salary. As for Martin, well, any university in the world would be delighted to employ him. He's spent most of his academic life studying theology and philosophy – he's going to be perfect.'

So it was agreed and Martin made his way to the new university. It was a sudden appointment. Martin had to leave without even speaking to some of his friends. And when he arrived in Wittenberg, he was thrown straight into lectures and studies. It had been some time since he had read any philosophy, so he had quite a bit to catch up on.

Preaching was also something new for him. Because it was a new university, the chapel had yet to be built. There were plans for one, a rather grand one, but when Martin began preaching, it was only the foundations that had been laid. A few feet of stone wall had gone up too – but that was it. Within the beginnings of the wall a little wooden chapel had been put up as a temporary worship place. Wooden planks propped up the walls and roof. It was somewhat dishevelled, but it did the job.

In 1510, Martin Luther was again requested to take on new duties. Staupitz had a plan.

'You're to go to Rome with Brother John. I'll accompany you as far as Heidelberg, but the plan is that you'll go by foot from there through Bavaria, stopping possibly at Füssen at the Tyrol pass and then into Italy. I think you could visit Milan, if you cross the Alps, passing near Lake Como.'

Luther was more than happy to travel to the Holy City of Rome. It was an honour to be chosen to represent the Order before the papal court.

'I know you understand the issues involved,' Staupitz pointed towards the letters that lay across his desk. 'Some of the other Augustinian convents[1] have protested against the recent reforms. You'll start the journey with ten gold florins – plenty to see you through to Rome, if you are careful. Food and lodging should be received, whenever possible, at monasteries.'

It was a long journey, one full of new experiences and visits. Some opened up Martin's eyes in new ways … such as the wonderful hospitals in Florence, where the poor and sick were graciously cared for. But he was disgusted at the luxury of some of the larger monasteries he visited, where monks feasted and drank in abundance.

---

1. A convent is either a community of priests, religious brothers/sisters, or nuns, or the building used by the community, particularly in the Roman Catholic Church.

When they reached the city of Rome, Martin felt like a long-lost son finally coming home. 'I greet thee, Holy Rome!' he called out, as he entered its gates.

It didn't take them long to get the legal business out of the way. Martin then took advantage of being in one of the most important cities in the world. He visited all the ancient monuments and churches that he could. He went to the Colosseum and the Baths of Diocletian. There was also a famous building that was said to be part of Pilate's house.

His companion had mentioned that if you climbed the stairs on your knees, you could claim an indulgence at the end – freedom from 1,000 years of penance in purgatory.

Purgatory was believed to be a place where people went before they entered heaven. It was somewhere people went after death, in order to be made pure and fit for heaven. Those who believed in purgatory believed that it was a place of great suffering, but if you did lots of good works you would spend less time there.

Luther began the long climb up the stairs, praying as he went, but halfway up he simply stopped himself. It was another point in his life where he realised he was mistaken in his beliefs. The words that had changed his life from the Book of Romans flashed across his mind:

'The just shall live by faith' (Romans 1:17).

'What are you doing?' Martin admonished himself. Rising from his knees he stood briefly, before making his way back down. He knew that there was no action he could do that would save him. There was nothing that he could do in order to get to heaven. Jesus Christ had done it all. Climbing stairs, penance – all of that was worth nothing.

Over time, Luther's thoughts and beliefs about many things changed. He now believed that only God could save you from your sin, and perhaps it is at this point that his beliefs about purgatory also changed. One by one, the false teachings of the church were beginning to lose their hold on him.

At the end of his stay, he made his way out through the same Roman gates that he had entered. His opinion of the city was now quite different. He had seen the corruption at the heart of the city and the church. He had seen gross misspending of money. He could see that the church of Rome and its leaders cared more about luxuries than God.

'If there is a hell,' he muttered, 'Rome is built over it.'

Martin was back at Wittenberg by 1512 and again Staupitz had plans for giving him more responsibilities. He could see how able Martin was and knew he would be a great Doctor of Theology.

'After the ceremony, you will be called Dr. Martin Luther, and after you are made a member of the university senate, I intend to step down as regent and you will take my place.'

Martin truly felt the honour of this and the challenge.

'The elector has agreed to pay for the expenses of your graduation,' Staupitz continued. 'My dear Martin, I am overjoyed to see how God has brought you to this point and I look forward to see how he will use you in the future.'

Martin began his work as Doctor of Theology by a series of talks, first on the Psalms and then the books of Romans and Galatians, which meant that again, he was brought back to the thoughts of justification – how it was that God alone brought sinners to salvation.

One of the Psalms he studied was Psalm 22, where one morning he read the line, 'My God, my God, why hast thou forsaken me?' (Psalm 22:1). These lines immediately reminded him of the words of Jesus on the cross. In his mind and soul, a fire was lit; again, he saw as plain as day what Jesus Christ had done, and how pathetic an attempt it was to secure your own salvation through good works. 'Christ has taken my sin and it is through Christ that my sin has been borne away. He was separated from God, though he did no sin. He was separated from God instead of me.'

Martin's continued study of Scripture fed into all his lectures and sermons.

The students were enthralled by what he had to say and soon the news spread – even the town's people began to attend. The Word of God took on new life as the people listened to Martin's lectures.

'That monk makes the Bible come alive for me!' exclaimed the old baker, as he left chapel one Lord's Day morning.

'Yes, the little proverbs and stories help you understand what the Bible really means,' his wife added.

'I used to think that the Bible was just for priests, but now I see that the people in the Bible are just like you and me really, so we should read it too. If only I could read.'

'I know! Though I can read German, I can't read Latin. But at least Dr. Luther is reading it to us and explaining it! That's something we've never had before.'

By 1516, Luther was given even more duties when he was made superintendant of eleven Augustinian convents. Even though this was a good promotion, Luther was beginning to see strong opposition to the way he did things.

'The way I see it,' he explained to Staupitz one day, 'is that they teach theology whereas I teach the Holy Scripture.'

The Doctors of Theology were teaching about what others thought about Scripture, about what others had written, not about God's Word itself. Preachers in the church preached more about what they imagined than about what God said.

Martin's whole life now centred on one thought – it was the fire in his belly, the thunder in his heart. 'God of his own free grace pardons sin for the sake of our Lord Jesus Christ. No man, however saintly, or pious, can work out his own salvation.'

Staupitz continued to listen to the reasoning of his younger friend.

'What I see so many lecturers teaching,' continued Martin, 'is pagan rather than Christian. They teach more of Aristotle than they do of St. Paul ... and the church supports this.'

Staupitz nodded sadly. It was true; both he and Martin struggled with this.

Something in Martin wanted to rise up and berate these teachers, these false prophets.

'It sickens me to see these lambs being led away by wolves,' he muttered.

There was one wolf in particular who had wandered into Luther's path ... a wolf dressed in monk's clothing, whose name was Tetzel.

A Wolf, a Hammer and
a Dispute

Martin had heard that the wolf, Tetzel, wasn't that far away. He was approaching the area of Meissen. On the coming Lord's Day, Martin fully intended to thunder against the pope's commissary Johann Tetzel. Martin chafed inside at the injustice, blasphemy, thievery and dishonesty of that man. His list went on. All of these dreadful things were being done in the name of Christ.

The church, you see, had invented a new way of supporting itself. It was, in fact, robbing the poor by indulgences. Martin had come across these before. Indulgences were promises from the pope. If you did certain tasks or said certain prayers, then the pope would promise to allow your soul easy access to heaven. You would spend less time in purgatory. It was all an example of how the church had created doctrines that had no real basis in the Bible. However, now these promises were being given to people if they paid money for them.

Martin had heard that even the elderly grandfather, who kept the garden of the university, had bought an indulgence the last time he was at Zerbst on market day. He and his wife could barely pay for their little hovel of a home, but they had scraped together enough coins to pay for one of Tetzel's indulgences. Tetzel was making his way around the country selling these scraps of paper to the ordinary people, making use of their fear of death and hell in order to gather money for the building of a grand new church in Rome.

Martin had spoken to the gardener and was upset to hear of his reasons for buying the indulgence in the first place. His young granddaughter was gravely ill. 'Our little darling shan't spend one more minute in purgatory than she has to,' the dear old man had sobbed.

Martin sighed and asked the old man how much he had spent on the indulgence. Going back to his rooms, he found enough coins to pay back the old man what he had spent. 'All this money to build a cathedral in Rome, over the bones of St. Peter, they say. We don't even know that St. Peter was buried there, not for sure. And I'm also not convinced the money is going to be spent on the cathedral, either. I've seen the corruption in Rome and the greed of the cardinals.'

Giving the old man the coins, he instructed him not to waste it on any more indulgences. 'Let me come and visit your granddaughter and I will pray with her. Tell her about the love of God and how forgiveness is free to anyone who trusts in Christ.'

With a tear in his eye, the old gardener nodded, thanking Luther for the money as he left.

Luther shook his head in astonishment at how the church was robbing poor men and women of their daily bread. 'Pope Leo himself says that all who buy these tickets or indulgences will be completely forgiven. Yet again, the church deceives the people. I must teach about how false these indulgences are. Tetzel says that an indulgence makes you share in all the good works of the godly saints, such as St. Anne and St. Elizabeth, even the Virgin Mary herself. What I have to remind my congregation is that they cannot buy salvation, nor work for it, either. We can only be certain of forgiveness of sins and life everlasting because it was purchased by Christ, not by our coins or any ticket.'

As he sat down at his desk to start the first draft of his sermon, he picked up a letter from one of the brothers who had witnessed Tetzel's performance in his own town. Martin was relieved to see that there were others just as disturbed as he was.

'The procession going past my window is full of pomp and ceremony. A red cross has already been put up in the square for all to see. The pope's banner blows in the wind outside and I can hear Tetzel's cry, "The soul flees out of purgatory as soon as the money rattles in the box. The red cross of the indulgence is of equal power as the cross of Christ." You might think they were receiving God himself instead of this villain.'

'He is right to call him a villain. That is why I must stand up to Tetzel,' Martin reasoned with himself. But in going against Tetzel, Martin was fully aware he was also going against the church, and he struggled with this. He saw it as his duty to support the church, but how could he when he could plainly see that the church was wrong?

Martin decided to make his complaints public by nailing them to the door of the Castle Church at Wittenberg. This was the place in town where you published important documents.

With hammer and nails in hand, Martin took his list or '95 Theses' as it would later be called, and nailed it to the door. It was on All Saints Day in 1517 – an important day in the church calendar – so many people saw his list as they took part in the celebrations.

Martin's Theses were a written argument. He wanted to show what was wrong with indulgences. He must have known what an uproar it would cause. Everyone wanted to read it. In fact, so many people wanted to read them that the space around the castle church was mobbed! Thankfully, the university had a printing press of its own, so copies were made and handed out. Soon there was a demand for more, as news spread about Martin's list. Requests were coming from all over Germany. Two weeks later, copies of the Theses had spread across the whole country, and within four weeks they were being read across the civilised world.

When Tetzel published a counter-argument, Luther's hot-headed students burnt whatever copies they could find. Much activity and discussion resulted from what Luther published. Soon people were discussing little else at hearths and taverns across Germany.

'Have you heard this? Can it be true?' one man asked another as he pointed out a phrase in Luther's Theses. 'It says, "When our Lord and Master Jesus Christ said, 'Repent,' he intended that the entire life of believers should be repentance. Repentance cannot be understood to mean the sacrament of penance, or the act of confession and satisfaction administered by the priests."'

'What? Does he mean that all those times I've been going to confession – it's simply been a waste of time?'

'I think so! But further on, he says, 'The pope cannot remit any guilt, except by declaring that it has been remitted by God."'

'Well, that monk has set the cat among the pigeons for certain. I don't think the pope is going to be too happy with him!'

'Here's another: "Christians should be taught that he who sees someone needy, but looks past him, and buys an indulgence instead, receives not the pope's remission, but God's wrath."'

The old gardener was also watching all the goings-on. Luther had been to visit his granddaughter and prayed with her.

'Doctor Luther speaks the truth,' he said to a friend, as they listened to a student from the university read from the '95 Theses'. 'Our only hope is Christ. The next time I see that red cross on market day, I will turn away from it, for sure!'

However, though many believed the Theses, there were those who didn't. This list of ninety-five complaints was just the start of something that would bring Martin into more discussion, argument and trouble!

A fortnight after the Theses had been published, Martin walked back past the Castle Church door quite early in the morning. His words were now back on the door, as well as being printed and published across the whole of Germany. Martin rubbed his head in bewilderment. The Theses were now being translated into other languages and sent abroad. 'It's not just Germany that hates this practice of indulgences,' Martin said to himself, as he looked around at the dirty streets, hearing the sounds of a small German town just waking up. It was amazing to think that what he had written was reaching so far, but still Martin had hoped for more. He wanted open debate, but so far no one was coming forward and Martin's bishop had instructed him to publish nothing more on the matter.

As he turned to walk back to his rooms, the bitter smell of smoke lingered in the air. Martin sighed with frustration. 'My students have been burning Tetzel's work again. They don't seem to realise that they're not helping me at all.'

Martin wanted a discussion that got to the heart of the theology, the real moral questions. As his students were going about burning anything that criticized their beloved Doctor Luther, all that Martin could do was preach the truth to the increasing number of people who avidly listened to his sermons.

In time, Martin would be given the opportunity to defend his Theses ... and that time came in April 1518. There was a General Assembly held at Heidelberg and, although many of Luther's friends felt it was foolhardy of him to leave the safety of Wittenberg, nothing could dissuade him from taking part. Elector Frederic gave Martin some protection because the monk had succeeded in bringing some level of fame to his university town. 'And although I disagree with him in the matter of indulgences,' the elector declared, 'I do believe Luther to be a pious man. So he shall be under my protection throughout the whole assembly.'

It seems that, though the elector didn't agree with Martin Luther, he was quite proud to have such a clever and important man as part of his university.

On his return, Martin looked invigorated and more relaxed than he had been in some time. He had enjoyed the robust discussions, of which there had been many, a lot more than he had at first anticipated. However, there was one great disappointment.

Passing a book to his friend Myconius, Martin asked glumly, 'Have you read this?'

Myconius nodded. 'Yes, Martin. *Obelisks* was written by John Eck.'

Martin's shoulders slumped slightly. 'I thought he was my friend. It appears that he is no longer. We are to be at each other's throats. He utterly despises my position on the indulgences. However, I must put it behind me and prepare for final publication of the

Theses. I plan to call it *Resolutiones*. It needs a lot of work, more explanation. I will of course send a copy to the pope when it is finished.'

Luther's friend raised an eyebrow in surprise. 'I doubt he will read it. By all accounts, His Holiness doesn't take doctrinal matters that seriously. He likes to enjoy himself. Other than that, I think his greatest concern is politics. Who will replace the Holy Roman Emperor, that sort of thing. He wants to control this country and all the others, so who replaces the emperor when he dies is very important.'

Martin said nothing in reply. Politics seemed to get into everything these days. It was frustrating for men like Martin, who saw the church and the nations in the vice-like grip of men who thirsted after power and who paid little, or no attention to the Word of God.

'Martin,' his friend continued, 'I think the pope would gladly leave you alone if you left him alone. He's really all for a quiet life.'

Martin grimaced. 'That may be true, but the Vatican is full of other more blood-thirsty opponents.'

'Mazzolini, you mean?'

Martin nodded. 'Sylvester Mazzolini, born in Prierio – they call him Prierias. He's a Dominican monk and has written against the Theses. He's asking the pope to 'End the heresy of this German monk.''

Myconius laughed as Martin attempted an Italian accent.

'It was probably his influence that meant the pope demanded that I come to Rome, but the elector has seen to it that any interrogation is to be done on German soil. Instead of being pulled off to Rome, I'm to present myself before the papal legate at Augsburg. Once I've done this last rewrite, I'll be off. The elector has given me some money for the journey and will provide me with a lawyer when I arrive there.'

Wittenberg, Augsburg then Leipzig

The journey to Augsburg was on foot and Martin arrived there on the 8th of October, 1518. The papal legate, Cardinal Cajetan, had two particular points to raise with Martin.

'Luther denies that those virtuous actions, done in the past by the saints, can be given, shared out, as it were, by the pope to the faithful. And he also denies that the sacraments[1] are effective, unless the recipient believed in Christ. We must put an end to this monk's heresies! If I can just persuade him to gently turn his back on all this troublesome talk.'

The cardinal subtly suggested that if Martin would give up on these two disagreements, the Vatican would turn a blind eye to all that gone on in Wittenberg. 'It will simply be forgotten,' the cardinal whispered into Luther's ear.

---

1. Sacraments in the Roman Catholic Church comprise of the Mass or what Protestants now refer to as the Lord's Supper; Baptism; Confirmation; Penance; Anointing of the Sick; Holy Orders and Matrimony. In the Reformed Protestant church there are two sacraments: The Lord's Supper and Baptism.

Martin frankly refused. 'The just shall live by faith!' He said it out loud as much to remind himself as to rebuke the cardinal.

Martin would not recant.

The cardinal was hopping mad! He wrote to Elector Frederic as soon as Martin left.

'You are sheltering a heretic,' he blustered as his secretary busily scratched the accusation across the parchment.

When Elector Frederic replied, he hit the nail on the head.

'You cannot accuse a man of heresy who no theologian in Germany has succeeded in showing to be in the wrong.'

Martin then made an appeal for his case to be heard before a council – and the emperor and the elector supported this idea.

In the meantime, the publication of Martin's Theses had given the monk a taste for writing and printing. Seeing the need to teach good theology and doctrine to the church, Martin reprinted the three great creeds: The Apostles'; The Nicene and the Athanasian. These were published in the German language, and Martin wrote his own introduction.

People who read these confessions and Martin's words had their eyes opened. The church was more than the pope! But who was going to tell the pope that? The pope wasn't listening. Representatives from Rome came to Germany to try and drown out the disagreements – or to shut Luther up.

Martin was willing to keep quiet if the dispute was referred for investigation to two prelates – Archbishop of Trier and the Bishop of Würzburg. 'But my opponents must also agree to be quiet,' Martin declared.

This didn't happen. Martin kept his end of the bargain, but his one-time friend Eck would not leave him alone.

The year 1520 would be crucial for Luther. 'You don't have a choice,' Philipp Melanchthon, another of Luther's close friends, urged him. 'Eck isn't going to let this go, Martin. You'll have to debate him face to face.'

Martin gathered some parchments and sighed.

'Where does he suggest this "discussion" should take place?' Martin asked.

'Leipzig,' was the reply. 'If we arrive there towards the 24th of June, that should be time enough before the dispute begins.'

This Leipzig Disputation was going to turn out to be yet another turning point in Luther's life.

A large group of professors and students from Wittenberg arrived at Leipzig on the 24th of June, 1520. The disputation would involve not only Luther, but another debater, Carlstadt. He would also have to face down John Eck.

Melanchthon accompanied Martin on the journey, and as they neared the end of the journey, Martin was filled in on some of the details of the dispute. 'Carstadt will be the first to debate Eck. Do you think he is up to it?'

'Why do you ask?' Martin looked up from the book he was reading.

'Oh, I don't know. He seems very nervous, and knowing Eck as we do ...'

Martin nodded. 'You're right, of course. Eck is brilliant. A theological professor at Ingolstadt, he is a very bright man indeed. He has studied everything I have written. He is very learned and a determined debater. I've locked horns with him before and know what to expect. Carlstadt doesn't.'

Melanchthon then went on to remind Martin that the dispute would start on the 26th, which would be the date when they would settle the terms for the dispute before beginning the debate in earnest on the 27th 'But because the university here doesn't have a room large enough, the duke has given us the use of the great hall in the castle called Pleissenburg ... oh, here we are, Martin. We've arrived at our lodgings.' And with that, Martin put his book away as the cart drew to a halt.

'I hope all those Wittenberg students will behave themselves while they are here.'

Melanchthon laughed at his friend's concerns. 'I'm sure they will. By all accounts, it's the Leipzig lot you have to watch out for. Apparently they can be quite tough.'

'Hmm,' Martin nodded his head. 'So that's why all the students have come with their spears and halberts.'

'Yes,' Melanchthon said, 'it's for our protection.'

'Makes us look good too,' Martin smiled. 'That might help.'

It appeared that everyone wanted to look good on this occasion. The grand hall was cleaned and furnished with two great chairs in prime position for the debaters to sit in. When everyone arrived at the church for the Mass, a brand new choir of twelve sweet choristers raised their voices in beautiful melody. A meal was prepared for all the dignitaries and delegates until finally, at 2 pm on the 27th, the debate began. It wasn't until the 4th of July that Martin Luther and John Eck faced each other across the floor. Carlstadt had not done that well against the seasoned debater. Some wondered how Martin would do. His close friends were quietly confident.

As the two men made their way towards the chairs, an excited murmuring could be heard in the hall.

'Both the sons of peasants, can you believe it?' one professor said in a whisper.

His young student looked on, slightly curious. 'I didn't know. But now that you come to think about it, Dr. Luther does have the look of "the country" about him.'

'What do you mean?'

'Well, he's not tall like the duke or the other dignitaries. Dr. Luther is rather short really. If you were being kind, you would describe him as being slender, but it would be more accurate to say he was emaciated.'

'Oh, really,' his professor protested, 'I think that's a bit too strong … but you can see his cheek bones … perhaps he studies too much. I heard that he used to fast a lot and that he still doesn't really eat enough.'

The student looked over to where the two debaters were approaching the chairs. 'Luther's voice always sounds clear and distinct. And he's generally polite and friendly. I never hear anyone complain about his manners. Even when his opponents try to rattle him, he stays calm.'

'That's true, but it could be different once this debate starts. I've seen Martin get hot under the collar once or twice. And I think that may be why he's holding a small bunch of flowers ... do you see, in his left hand. I've seen him sniff them once or twice already.'

At this point, Melanchthon joined in the conversation. 'I think the flowers calm him down a little. But I believe that Luther's presence of mind and his competence will be what brings him through this debate ... and his trust in God. But I'd like to hear what both of you think of John Eck.'

The young man looked at the opponent. 'Large. Square. A strong voice ... comes from his chest. Somewhat harsh. Again, he doesn't look like the dukes and dignitaries. His body is more suited to a butcher than a theologian.'

The professor and Melanchthon laughed at this observation.

'But what's the whole point of this debate?' one student asked, a bit puzzled. He had obviously not been listening to anything that had been going on.

'It's really about the supremacy of the church,' Melanchthon summed up quickly. 'Luther says the

Word of God has more authority than the pope … but hush now. It looks as though things are about to start in earnest.'

'Yes, let's see how the peasants do in their debate,' someone whispered. And they all settled down to listen. The debate would last five whole days!

Martin's friends had been confident he would do well. But on his return to Wittenberg, Martin felt depressed and weary. In his opinion, the debate had not gone well for him. To deal with his disappointment, Martin threw himself into his work at the university, and into his preaching.

'The people need me,' he insisted to Melanchthon. 'The students, too.'

'Well, do that then … get back to your congregation and the university, but don't give up. Prepare what was said at the disputation for publication. The country, the world even, needs to read your arguments. In print, people may have quite a different opinion of the debate. Eck is a blusterer and clever with his tactics. Take time to complete your argument against the pope. They may think the battle has been won … but …'

'I think they might be right … all the pope can do now is excommunicate me as a heretic – kick me out of the church.'

Kicked out, but still Writing

Martin was kicked out of the church. He felt as though he was being pushed and pulled in multiple directions. Even though it all seemed to be a large setback, Martin did eventually realise that not every victory is a victory and not every defeat a defeat. Sometimes defeats are victories.

The Leipzig Disputation was indeed the point at which Luther was pushed out of the church – and this brought new words from Luther's pulpit and Luther's pen ... and the people could talk of little else.

'Did you hear that Luther has been excommunicated?'

'Yes, I did. They've finally shown their real colours. Germany for the Germans, that's what I say. Why should these people in Rome tell us what to do? Why should we send them all our money?'

'Absolutely! Luther speaks the truth. I've heard, that because of all the money we have sent to Rome, our own German church is in poverty, and the artisans and the peasants are all worse off because they're building palaces in Rome for cardinals and their illegitimate offspring!'

'Yes. They claim to be so moral and pure, but they're just hypocrites.'

Conversations like this took place in homes and meeting houses all over Germany. Even in castles, men like Ulrich von Hutten and Franz von Sickingen studied Luther's writings regularly. 'Does anyone dare try to undermine Luther's doctrines or think that he can if he tries?' Sickingen wrote in a letter one day.

And that was one of the big changes Martin found in his everyday life since the disputation. 'Everyone is writing me letters,' he exclaimed, as Melanchthon came through the door with the latest pile of post.

'I think it is time for you to write a book,' his friend replied.

Martin agreed. 'A book would address all these questions without this repetitive task of letter writing.'

'Just think,' Melanchthon pointed out. 'If Leipzig hadn't happened, if you hadn't debated with John Eck, how different your life would be now.'

'It would be a lot quieter,' Martin grinned, 'but yes, I know for a fact now that the church and our nation of Germany need reform. Our first step has to be a separation from Rome.'

'You're not talking about a revolution though, are you?' Melanchthon asked.

'No. You know I don't agree with that. This kind of change can't happen with the sword. We need genuine religion to spread across the whole population.'

'That's a huge task.'

'But not so difficult as it would have been in previous generations. We have the printing press now.'

'Yes, and how you make use of it! I've heard that in 1517, thirty-seven books were printed in the German language and that in 1518, that rose to seventy-one – no less than twenty of those titles were from your pen. In 1520, we've had 208 German language books published, and 133 of those were yours!'

Yes, Martin had certainly adopted the new technology of printing and made it his own.

Publishers and printers liked it when Martin Luther wrote a book or pamphlet. Martin wrote German books for German people. These books reached out to ordinary German readers – and the books were on the whole short. This meant that they were less expensive to produce, cheap for the reader to buy and therefore made the printers and publishers something called 'profit'! Martin, however, made very little money from his writing. He was more concerned about the message these books contained than the money they could make him.

And they could have made him quite a bit of money, because the whole of Germany was eager to find out what Luther thought.

If the disputation in Leipzig hadn't happened, Martin would probably never have published all these books. Martin actually felt that he had a clearer view of what he actually believed in now. He was more convinced than ever that it was God's work and God's work alone that saved sinners, and that the monastic life was more of a hindrance than a help to faith.

Luther's tract *On Christian Liberty* begins with these words:

> 'A Christian man is the most free lord of all and subject to none; a Christian man is the most dutiful servant of all and subject to everyone.'[1]

Martin wanted Germany to be free from Rome. He wanted the church to be free from the pope, yet he knew that all Christians, though free, also had duties to obey God's Word and love their fellow man.

> 'It does not profit the soul to wear sacred vestments or to dwell in sacred places nor does it harm the soul to be clothed in worldly raiment and to eat and drink in the ordinary fashion. The soul can do without everything except the Word of God, and the Word of God is the Gospel of God concerning his Son.'[2]

Martin wrote and spoke and continually brought people back to God's Word. For example, he didn't think it was right to use words like 'pope' and 'clergy'. He pointed out that the Bible only used words like 'ministers' and 'servants', but didn't use words such as 'cardinals' or 'bishops'.

---

1. From a tract *On Christian Liberty* by Martin Luther.

2. From a tract *On Christian Liberty* by Martin Luther.

Scribbling some notes at his desk, he thought about the words people used for their work and jobs ... shepherds, bakers, carpenters ... 'Men and women who live like that in the family, workshop and in the ordinary world have as direct a vocation from God as any monk ... perhaps more so. Often, the monk can be mistaken in thinking that he is the only one with a religious life. If I can deliver ordinary men and women from a fear of priests and popes, what a deliverance that would be.

I must also point out to the people that if you have faith, you have everything. If you don't have faith, nothing else will satisfy you. And then they must see that everything a Christian does must come from his faith. Someone may find it necessary to fast and perform acts of divine service, but these are not good works in themselves; they do not make you good. But rather the good works that you do are signs that you love and trust God. So they are to be done with a joyful spirit for God!'

Martin's next book insisted that everything be brought to the test of the authority of the Word of God. 'The Roman Church has held the church captive to human traditions and the commandments of men,' Martin wrote urgently. 'These run counter to the plain messages and promises of the Word of God.'

Martin's study of Scripture brought him to understand God's Word in a way that he hadn't before, and it impacted his own life and the life of others in crucial ways.

He made a point of saying in his address *To The Nobility of the German Nation respecting the Reformation of the Christian Estate* that he believed it was quite alright for priests to marry, as there was nothing in the Bible that forbade it. He pointed out that all natural relationships in the family and home, and in the honest work of the tradesman and the profession of the nobleman were of equal value and spirituality. He was beginning to sound less and less like a monk.

In the same publication, he spoke vehemently against the pope and his claims to be the only one who could interpret Scripture. He railed against the church authorities and its corruption, describing them as wolves in wait for sheep. 'Do we still wonder why princes, noblemen, cities, foundations, convents, and people grow poor? We should rather wonder that we have anything to eat.'

There were many issues that he addressed when he put pen to paper. He even said that if someone wished to leave a convent or monastery, they should be allowed to do so. 'God will accept voluntary service only,' was Martin's opinion.

And while all this writing was going on, the pope was doing some writing of his own. A papal 'bull' was being prepared – a document that condemned Luther for his criticisms of the church and its officers. The pope then said that if Luther recanted, he would be welcomed back into the church with open arms. But if Luther refused, then he would be treated like a heretic.

These words were pretty much a threat to Martin's life and could have caused his friends and colleagues to abandon him for fear for their own safety, but the University of Wittenberg took no notice of the pope's words. They ignored them completely. It had no effect on the people of that town, not one bit. Elector Frederic, after some consultation with people like Erasmus of Rotterdam, decided to protect Luther in order that he would, in the end, receive a fair trial. So as a result, Martin was able to continue preaching and teaching, and writing profusely.

Even with all this animosity from Rome, Martin seemed to gain more fire in his pen and in his beliefs. One day, he took the copy of the papal bull and set it ablaze. As the flames licked around the parchment and seal, it was evident that a new world was on the horizon. And Martin was in the thick of it!

The Diet of Worms

Now, there are two words that you're going to hear quite a bit in this chapter and you're definitely going to think that the two words together sound quite strange. Those words are Diet and Worms – but fear not when we use the word 'diet', it doesn't mean eating fewer calories, and it's certainly not about eating small wriggly creatures.

A diet in Martin Luther's time was an Imperial council meeting. It was when the rulers and authorities of all the nations, connected to the Holy Roman Empire, gathered together to decide on the important political and religious issues of the day. These diets, much like meetings of parliament or government today, would be held in different cities across the realm and were important events. The heads of state, princes, kings and the church leaders all attended.

In 1521, the diet was to be held in the city of Worms in Germany. Several issues were to be debated, but the main reason that this diet was being held was to sort out the issue of Martin Luther.

The world was on the cusp of new beginnings. The Holy Roman Empire had recently enthroned a new emperor, a young man of nineteen, Charles V. He had considerable power already, being the King of Spain as well as having states in the Netherlands.

Because Martin had disagreed fundamentally with the doctrines of the Roman Catholic Church, and had made his disagreements public through the Theses, the emperor was summoning Martin Luther to stand before the heads of state and the religious authorities to answer for his 'crimes'. The fact that he had publicly burnt a copy of the papal bull had just added fuel to the already raging fire.

Charles V wanted to bring the now changing world back to the days when the empire had been at its strongest and in order to do this, in his eyes, he had to restore the pope to his position of ultimate power. The 'German monk' was attacking this power. He had to be sorted out. But the German princes didn't want 'one of their own' to go down without giving him the opportunity of a just hearing. Though several of the German rulers didn't agree with Martin Luther's teachings, they at least felt he should be allowed to speak for himself.

One thing concerned Martin when he received the summons to the Diet of Worms. Everything seemed to be stacking up against him: the papal bull, being summoned to defend himself before the rulers of the empire ... it could even mean that as well as excommunication, he could face execution.

'At least I have been promised a safe passage to Worms,' he muttered to himself, as he held the documents that had just been delivered to him by the Imperial herald.

'You're to appeal at the city of Worms no later than the 16th of April, 1521,' was the sharp instruction.

Martin nodded his head and calmly went back to his desk. There was another sermon he could finish in the meantime.

On the 2nd of April, he left in a large cart, provided for him by the people of Wittenberg. His companions for the journey were three men, one was a brother from the order, another was Martin's friend, Nicholas Amsdorf, and a young nobleman, Peter Staven, a student from the university.

The cart was well covered by canvas and fairly comfortable underneath with a thick layer of hay.

Just before their departure, Martin scribbled the final lines of a letter, encouraging another friend to be brave:

> 'I know and am certain that our Lord Jesus Christ still lives and rules. Upon this knowledge and assurance I rely, and therefore I will not fear ten thousand popes; for he who is with me is greater than he who is in the world.'[1]

His great friend, Melanchthon, was very upset to see Martin leave. As Martin waved goodbye, he spoke the following words:

---

1. Lindsay, Thomas, *Martin Luther: The Man Who Started the Reformation*, Christian Focus Publications, 2008.

'Dear brother, if I don't come back, if my enemies put me to death, you will go on teaching and standing fast in the truth; if you live, my death will matter little.'[2]

And then they set off – a little band of men, but before them went a herald with a yellow banner, blazoned with the black two-headed Imperial eagle. Martin Luther may have been a wanted man, and may have been summoned by the emperor, yet he was under that monarch's protection. It was plain for all to see. Anyone who planned to assault this particular pilgrim took a huge risk.

Many who saw the cart and the herald rushed out to see the now famous Martin Luther on what they thought would be his last journey. At Erfurt, when they arrived there, Martin preached to a great crowd on the text from John 20:19-20, 'Peace be unto you; and when he had said so, he shewed unto them his hands and his side.'

Their journey took them through some familiar territory, such as Leipzig and even through Eisenach. Finally, the cart trundled through Friedberg, Frankfurt and Oppenheim, before arriving at the city of Worms.

It was a long and tiring journey, but throughout, Martin's courage never left him. And the stories of the crowds that came out to greet him went ahead of him to Worms. The papal supporters became concerned,

2. Lindsay, Thomas, *Martin Luther: The Man Who Started the Reformation*, Christian Focus Publications, 2008.

and some thought that perhaps it might be best to ensure that Martin never reached Worms in the first place. They tried to persuade him to compromise, reminding him of another reformer, John Huss, who had been burnt at the stake. But now that Martin was on his way, nothing would dissuade him.

'I will go to Worms if there are as many devils there as tiles on the roofs. Huss was burnt, but the truth was not burnt with him.'

When Martin's little group finally made their way into the city, a group of knights arrived to give them safe passage, and they were escorted to their lodgings. For safety, they were situated right next door to Elector Frederic. The German prince wanted to be certain that this monk of his would be protected.

The following day, Martin was summoned before the Diet. The emperor sat on his throne, where below him the six electors of Germany sat in their own chairs. The hall was filled with other princes and church officers, and on a table, at the front, sat a pile of Luther's books. Martin shivered. He had never been in such a company of people before. He was asked if he was the writer of the books that lay before him. And if so, did he stand by the words that he had written, or would he recant?

Martin swallowed. His voice came out, but weakly. 'If you will please give me a moment to consider my answer.'

He was given to the following day.

Martin immediately went back to his lodging. His heart was pumping. His head was spinning.

'What am I to do?'

Pacing the floor from sundown to sunrise, Martin spent much of that night in desperate prayer. By morning, when the birds were breaking into song, Martin had broken with his conflict.

It was the evening of the 18th of April when Martin was again summoned before the court. People thronged the streets in order to catch a glimpse of him. It was so busy that they had to take side streets in order to get Martin to the hall, which itself was so full that the electors had to push their way to get to the front. The table of books still sat there from the day before. But this time, Luther was ready with his response. His voice was stronger. He was calm.

Again, Luther was asked if these books were his and if he was willing to defend them or recant.

Martin took a deep breath and began his defence in German.

He slowly, but surely, pointed out that not all of his books were the same. In some of them he had dealt with matters of faith and morals. And as far as he could ascertain, nobody had made any complaints about these.

'Now, other titles are against the papacy, whose doctrine and example are the ruination of Christendom. If I were to retract these books, then this would only strengthen its odious tyranny. There are some other books where perhaps I have been over-vehement in my attack, in a way unbecoming of a Christian. But I am not willing to recant these words either. But if anyone is willing to show me where I have erred, I am willing to listen.'

Because the emperor didn't understand German, Martin had to then repeat all his arguments in Latin. In all, the discussion took a good two hours before it was finished. And then the emperor, through a translator, told Martin to give a plain answer – 'Will you retract all that you have said contradicting the decisions of the Council of Constance?' (The Council of Constance was a diet that had met some hundred years earlier and had made decisions that Martin's writings were disagreed with). 'If you will, you will be dealt with leniently.'

Martin replied, 'I must be convinced either by the testimony of Scripture or by clear arguments. I cannot trust the pope or councils by themselves, since it is as clear as daylight that they have not only erred, but contradicted themselves. I am bound by the Scriptures which I have quoted; my conscience is united to the Word of God. I may not and will not recant, because to act against conscience is neither honest nor safe.'

Pausing, he then added, 'I can do nothing else; here I stand, so help me God! Amen.'

After some further questions, the emperor, frustrated and annoyed, dismissed the room and sent Martin back to his lodgings, escorted by a troop of guards. When the people on the street saw this, they thought that Martin was being taken to prison and would have begun a riot, had not Martin calmly addressed them, calming the situation down.

The following day, the emperor wished to proceed with Martin's condemnation, but the Germans involved in the diet asked for a delay. It was felt that perhaps further negotiations could take place with Martin and that maybe he could yet be persuaded to compromise. But whenever any of these discussions took place, they always broke down whenever Martin was asked to submit himself to any authority other than Holy Scripture.

While all this was going on, Martin was never far away from his pen. Yet again, he took the opportunity to write and publish. The printers sent out the papers that Martin wrote, all across Germany and the people more and more looked on him as their hero. Luther's books were now being sold openly at every street corner and marketplace.

Though the emperor, pope and their followers wished to see Martin put to death, a great uprising of Christians from many backgrounds, classes and countries were rising up in defence of Brother Luther.

Brother John came running into their lodgings one afternoon, with the news that a placard had been found posted up on the walls of the town hall.

'What sort of placard?' Nicholas asked, 'and why are you in such a fluster about it?'

'It's not just any old placard,' Brother John retorted. 'It declares that there are 400 knights with 800 men at arms who have bound themselves to take vengeance if Luther is in any way harmed. Nobody has signed it, but I can tell you people are taking notice of it. It has put fear into the hearts of the noblemen. I won't be surprised if they let Luther go soon.'

Nicholas sighed with relief. 'Back to Wittenberg ... I must say, I'll be glad to get home. But I don't know if it will be as easy as all that.'

And though the emperor gave permission for Luther to return, Nicholas was right. Deals were being made behind the scene. The pope was so keen put an end to the 'Luther' problem, he was willing to do certain things for the emperor as long as he put Luther down. The emperor agreed to the terms and with some deceptive tactics, managed to get the ban against Luther signed and delivered.

Some clever wording in the ban ensured that Luther had twenty days' safe conduct after his departure from Worms, but from then on nobody was allowed to give Luther any 'house, or home, food, drink or shelter, by words or deeds.'[3]

It stopped short of demanding his death. But if anybody did have leanings that way, the pope and the emperor wouldn't have stopped them.

However, if someone had wanted to kill Luther, they would have to find him first.

And that was the strange thing! Nobody could work out where he was.

It was as if Martin Luther had disappeared off the face of the earth.

---

3. Lindsay, Thomas, *Martin Luther: The Man Who Started the Reformation*, Christian Focus Publications, 2008.

Captured, but not Captive

Luther sat in the covered cart that he had arrived in; the same travelling companions were with him, bumping around on the hay as they trundled over pot holes and tree roots. Travelling by cart was never that comfortable. It was, however, somewhat better than riding on horseback, exposed to the elements. As they made their way out of Worms and back along the route they had taken, Martin was relieved to be making his way back to studies and university, although he was still uncertain about what the outcome of this whole excursion to Worms would be.

'I see the herald isn't with us this time,' Martin observed.

'Oh, he's here,' Nicholas pointed out, 'at the rear. We felt that it might be best not to draw attention to ourselves as we travel this time. We're going to be a bit quieter.'

Martin nodded. That was a good idea. To draw attention to themselves at this critical, dangerous point would be foolhardy.

After making their way through Eisenach, they stopped off at Möhra, where Martin had some relatives. After preaching in the parish church there in the morning, Martin then left on the afternoon of the 4th of May heading towards Gotha. About two miles east of Altenstein Castle, the road began to wind through some wooded slopes. A stream ran alongside their path, which took them past the ruins of a wayside chapel.

It was a quiet, peaceful scene, Martin noted as he looked through the canvas covering, only to hear the thunder of hoof beats in the distance. He also caught a glimpse of a flash of steel.

'Are we being pursued?' Martin asked anxiously.

Suddenly, the cart driver yelled out, raising his whip to the backs of the horses to make them speed up.

'Brigands!' he yelled, as he vainly tried to flee the oncoming attackers.

It all happened so quickly. Martin had no idea what was going on. Two knights on horseback dashed at the cart, ordering the driver to stop. A long lance, pointed at the driver's neck, soon brought him to a halt, and Martin was dragged from the cart and flung across the back of one of the mounts. As they galloped off into the distance, Martin's friends could only look on in shock. One of them reached down to the ground to pick up the grey felt hat that had fallen from Martin's head in the struggle.

Some way down the woodland path, Martin was released from the strong grip of a knight and placed onto his own horse before they set off again – where to, Martin couldn't say. At eleven o'clock that night, Martin found himself being ushered through the gates of a castle, where a kindly old gentleman approached him, smiling and uttering words of welcome.

'Have I been kidnapped, only to be treated like a duke?' Martin was puzzled.

The kindly old gentleman laughed a little at Martin's bewildered expression.

'Good evening, my friend. Good evening and welcome to the castle called Wartburg. Your good and kind Elector Frederic has seen to all this. Wittenberg will be too dangerous for you, so he rather cleverly arranged your kidnap! Wartburg will be your home now, so let me show you to your rooms.'

Martin was now in hiding – and would be for ten whole months.

None of his friends, not even Martin himself, had been in on the plan. Martin had to admit, however, that the elector's plan had been ingenious.

There were some changes he would have to get used to – his monk's habit was disposed of and instead he was dressed in knight's clothing. He was even given a new name, Knight George, and over time he grew his hair back and even grew a beard. He looked nothing like the rebel monk who was on the run from the pope and the emperor.

These changes were awkward at first, but then Martin began to enjoy his life at the castle. Sometimes he was allowed out on horseback for a ride through the forests, but what he really enjoyed was the peace and solitude he was allowed – and he put it to good use, composing hymns and translating the New Testament from Greek into German. It was something he had always longed to do – to give ordinary German folk the opportunity to read God's Word. And with Martin's poetic turn of phrase and common touch, he did just that.

However, he battled with his translation, using the original Greek texts. Sometimes Martin would scratch out a sentence he was particularly unhappy with fifteen times. It was important to get just the right wording. 'You have to ask the mother in the home, the children on the street, and the common man in the marketplace to see how they speak, and then use their words to make them understand.'

But it was in these struggles with translation that Martin would find himself most encouraged. Sometimes despondent in the gloomy castle, away from his friends and students, he would get depressed and morose. In his solitary life there, his imagination would sometimes overwork itself. Were it not for his task of getting the Word of God into the hearts and minds of his own people, he might have gone mad.

In September 1522, the first edition of the German New Testament was published, the fruit of Martin's endeavours in the room hidden away in the Wartburg. By December it had been sold out, and a second edition was needed.

'If only this one book would be in every language, in every hand and in the eyes, ears and hearts of all people!' Martin exclaimed.

While he was in Wartburg, Martin was still in touch with friends who, on occasion, were allowed to visit him in secret. Martin was also allowed to receive letters and send them, so he was not completely out of touch with the rest of the world. Sometimes he heard good news.

'I see that several parish priests have now married,' Martin mused as he read a scribbled note from one of the professors at Wittenberg. 'I am glad for them – it is a good choice that they have made.'

But he also heard bad news. There was an archdeacon, Carlstadt, who was causing trouble. It seemed that all the Reformation had gone to his head and that he had begun to take things too far. He had made the decision that all human learning was unnecessary – university and school. He and a few other hot-heads were causing trouble in Wittenberg. Luther became so anxious about it that he secretly paid a visit to the university town, hiding in his friend Nicholas Amsdorf's house. He returned to Wartburg greatly depressed with the situation. If it wasn't one group of people fighting to take him and the Reformation down, it was another group fighting to destroy everyone else. Martin begged the elector to allow him to return to Wittenberg. 'You do not need to protect me anymore from the Imperial officials.'

After his ten months of disguise as Knight George, Martin Luther was back in Wittenberg, getting the university and the schools back in order. Martin knew that not everyone could immediately follow all the new ideas he proposed. For example, the Mass – he wanted the people to partake of the bread and the wine. He just couldn't force people to do this. So he had two altars: one where the people could take the bread only, and another where they would take bread and wine. Over time, all the people moved over to the altar where both were offered. Everything happened peaceably, which was what Luther wanted.

Martin hoped for a gentle spread of the Reformation through Germany. He wanted unity and peace, yet this sort of peace was not what the people in Germany really wanted, not now that they had tasted freedom and what it meant. Martin didn't realise it yet, but his words of fire would be used against him in a terrible way during the Peasants' War, but in the meantime his thoughts began to move towards unity of a different sort.

'From another happily married priest, Martin,' his young secretary smiled, as he placed yet another letter on the pile.

Martin was busy replying to letters from all over Germany, while also holding a tutorial with some students who wished to discuss some theological points with the learned professor.

Martin nodded. He was getting a lot of that sort of letter lately. 'It is good that now the home life of the parish priest can be held up as an example to his parishioners. '

'Have you ever thought about marriage, Dr Luther?' his young assistant asked, perhaps with a little glint in his eye.

'No,' Martin said, emphatically. 'I have no desire for marriage. Priests need not practice celibacy if they don't want to. If they prefer a married life, then they can. Sometimes men and women are forced to take monastic vows in their early years, before they were called to that way of life, so I believe that they must then be at liberty to leave the cloister. However, men like myself who have deliberately taken these vows ought to keep them.'

'But you admit, Dr Luther, that you took those vows under the false impression that they would save your soul,' one of his more argumentative students piped up.

'Oh! How you young men do argue with me sometimes. This is my final word on the matter. I am not going to break those vows. I know I no longer wear my monastic robes. However, I'm not going to jettison everything from my life as a monk. I am quite fine as a bachelor, thank you!'

'Mmm …' one of the students looked on with some doubt. He had heard that his professor's eating habits were atrocious, his bed damp and flea-ridden! Dr. Luther was not fine as a bachelor! Perhaps it would be better for Dr. Luther to spend a little less time in tutorials and more time match-making for himself.

The student wondered, though, if there would be any woman willing to take on such a challenge!

He needn't have been concerned, as in the spring of 1523, Luther's writings found their way into a convent of Cistercian nuns, not that far from Leipzig. His words were causing quite a stir amongst some of the young women there. Many of them were of noble birth and had been left in the convent as very young women, until they had reached an age where they could take vows.

One of the nuns, a woman called Catherine von Bora, was convinced that the vows they had taken were unlawful.

'How old were you when they placed you in the convent?'

A pale-faced young nun screwed up her face as she tried to remember, 'It was so long ago, but I could have been six or seven, I think.'

'And you?' Catherine asked another.

'I was a bit older, eight maybe.'

'Well, it's my opinion that we were all put in here far too young. We've all made vows, but we wish to return to our homes. However, none of our families are willing to take us back.'

'Can you blame them?' another young women interrupted. 'If they did, they would be breaking the law. It would be a disgrace for them to have a runaway nun in the family.'

'Our only option is to write to this man, Luther. We need to explain our situation to him and ask for his help.'

Sometime later, after Luther had received the letter, a plan was put into action – daring, and actually a bit scandalous.

The nine young women at the convent all gathered to meet in Catherine's room.

One by one, the nuns squeezed through the window and noiselessly dropped to the courtyard below – a short drop, thankfully. Once all nine were on the ground, they quickly ran over to the wall, where a man was waiting to help them over. He then assisted each girl inside a large barrel on his cart. Some smelt of beer, others of fish. It all made for a rather unpleasant three-day journey. But it was worth it to escape the imprisonment of the convent.

Their final destination was Wittenberg, where Martin found each one of them a safe home with respectable local families.

Soon, the news of the convent breakout had spread everywhere.

'Well, Martin, I don't think you expected it would be widely supported. But I'm telling you, there are a lot of angry people out there. They can't believe what you've done,' Melanchthon declared.

Martin declared, 'People need to know what it's really like in the cloister for these young women. They have no idea. This is not a voluntary service they take part in – they are forced into it.'

Melanchthon nodded. 'Yes, I agree, Martin, but what are we going to do with these young women now that they are here?'

'Marry them off? I think I've got a list here somewhere of several potential suitors, all godly men, some of them noblemen, some of them priests – they all want good wives. We've got nine of them.'

So, from that day on, quite a bit of time in Martin's day was devoted to match-making the runaway nuns with potential husbands.

For the most part it went well, but there was one girl who was being a bit awkward. Her family had emphatically said they wanted nothing more to do with her, and no matter who they suggested to her as a potential mate, she turned them down.

'I'm sorry to say, but Catherine is just being difficult,' Dr Reichenbach apologised to Martin, as he visited him in his offices. 'Everyone we suggest, she turns down, and now she says she will not marry at all unless she is married to either Nicholas Amsdorf or ...' he paused ...

Martin asked, 'Or whom?'

'Or you.'

Martin was astonished.

Frau Doctor

Nothing is really known about what happened next, how Martin made his decision and what his words were. But it was very shortly after Catherine had made her proposal that she and Martin became husband and wife.

At some point, Martin confessed that he didn't marry for love – that certainly came later – but that he possibly married only because he realised it would really annoy the pope!

A fortnight after the ceremony and the wedding breakfast, a feast was given, to which the couple's relatives and distant friends were invited. Martin was overjoyed to see both his father and his mother at the event. His father's familiar firm embrace, almost squeezing all the air out of Martin's lungs, was all the proof he needed. Martin knew he was at last forgiven for his foolishness of being a monk.

An old Augustinian convent was given to Luther as a house, where Catherine soon set about sorting out the meals, the bedding and even Luther's rather badly organised finances.

Melanchthon grinned as he watched the young twenty-six-year-old Catherine take on the project of the forty-two-year-old Luther. He hadn't been supportive of Luther's plan of marriage originally and had even refused to attend the ceremonies, fearing that it would all amount to a huge scandal which would only harm the cause of the Reformation. But now he was beginning to see differently. Having been married himself a few years earlier, he could now see that marriage was good for himself and for his friend.

'He's even out tending to the garden!' he exclaimed.

And at the end of many of Luther's letters to his learned friends across the country, there would now often be a postscript in which he would pass on the requests of his young wife for melons or radish seeds. When their firstborn son, Hans, came along, the postscripts to his letters often included stories about the little lad who would be running around their house, getting into every corner of his father's study.

Letters to Catherine herself from Luther often began with terms of deep affection, 'My sweetheart', 'My dearly beloved' or 'My true love'. But it wasn't just her sweet face and pigtails that he liked; he appreciated her intelligence and common sense too, and sometimes would reflect this in his letters by referring to her as 'Frau Doctor.'

Just a year or so after his little boy's birth, Luther fell seriously ill. The baby brought him great comfort, but whenever he looked at him, he felt tears prick his eyelids as he thought about how he must leave behind a widow and a young child, unprovided for.

Catherine's strong words to him, as he lay on his sick bed, gave him great courage.

'If it be God's will, then I also choose that you be with him rather than with me. It is not so much I and my child that need you, as the multitude of pious Christian people. Take no thought for me.'

But after Martin's recovery, the plague arrived. Martin refused to leave, even though the new elector, Duke John, urged him to do so. Martin would not leave his flock. He remained in Wittenberg with his wife and child, and a new baby on the way.

Martin counted eighteen new graves at the Elster Gate one morning, just a stone's throw from their house. He was even present when the very first victim died. It started attacking his friends, and one dreadful morning it seemed to have attacked young Hans. However, his speedy recovery was a sign that it wasn't the plague, but some other childhood illness. When Catherine gave birth to their daughter, Elizabeth, the plague started to dissipate. But this good news was almost wiped out by the tragic news of more persecution of reformers throughout Germany. A letter arrived that told Martin that Leonard Kaiser had been burnt at the stake in Bavaria. In his turmoil and heartache, Martin took up his pen once more to write the following words:

'A safe stronghold our God is still,
A trusty shield and weapon;

He'll help us clear from all the ill
That hath us now o'ertaken.'[1]

When the plague ceased, none of Martin's family were among the corpses buried by the Elster Gate. For this he was truly thankful. The students and university professors were now beginning to make their way back to Wittenberg; studies would soon begin again. Martin sighed with relief. Lifting little Hans up, he swung him from side to side, like a pendulum. How this brought back memories of his own father.

Turning to Catherine, who was stirring something aromatic and delicious on the stove, Martin said, 'We should plan Elizabeth's baptism.'

Looking up with a smile, Catherine nodded with agreement and mentally started working out which rooms in the dilapidated old convent building needed repairs first.

When Luther's parents came to visit their son just before the baptism, Luther was pleased to show his father around. One or two of the worst rooms had been cleaned out and the windows repaired. The terrible drafts had for the most part been stopped.

'There is still much work to be done, but we will proceed as and when we have need. Right now, we have all the rooms we require. When more children arrive, God willing, we will repair the other rooms.' Martin drew his father's attention to the large garden that he and Catherine enjoyed taking care of.

---

1. *Ein' feste Burgist unser Gott*, words and music, Martin Luther, 1529.

Hans Luther smiled, but not at the garden or the view ... simply at the comment his son had made, that, God willing, there would be more children. Ruffling the hair of his little grandson, who was one of the old man's greatest pleasures ... one he had thought would never happen. He silently thanked the Lord for the blessing of family, and for the blessing he could now see his son would be to the church.

'I had such plans for you, my son,' he said to Martin, as he passed his little grandson a nut out of his pocket. 'It was to be the law for you, Martin, and then you became a monk. We had no plans, your mother and I, that you would ever go into the church as a career. But now I can see that God's thoughts are not our thoughts and his ways are not our ways. The Lord has made you into his servant and he has allowed us to be grandparents!'

The father and son, once estranged, now embraced, while the youngest Luther stuffed the nut in his mouth, crunched it, chewed it – then swallowed, wondering if there might be more.

Martin was glad to be reconciled with his parents. The joy the elderly couple had in their grandchildren was beautiful to behold. Martin rejoiced at the reunited family. 'This frail man and woman who brought me up, guarded me and sought my very best, may not be with us much longer.'

Indeed, Hans Luther passed away in 1530 and Margarethe a year later. At least they had seen their son begin his life away from the monastery, in a family of his own, at the commencement of a reformation of the church which they never dared dream of.

Over the coming years, there were great struggles. The country of Germany went through unsettled times. There were times of internal strife and revolts in the upper and lower classes of the nation. Martin found those times greatly stressful and when the fighting of the Peasants' War came to an end, Martin was not the same. If he had not had a wife and family, he may not have coped with it at all.

As it was, he had Catherine, three sons and two daughters. Other people also joined their household. Catherine's aunt had also been in the convent, but had not left with the women at the time Catherine escaped. However, eventually, she joined the Luther household, along with two orphan nieces, Lene and Else Kaufmann, who had been born to one of Luther's sisters. Another young girl called Anna Strauss joined the group and then, in addition, Luther allowed several students to board with them. It was quite a large house, after all. It meant that meal times were big, rather bustling affairs, with lots of talk.

As the last dinner dishes and tankards had been cleared away, Catherine took off her apron and settled herself down by the fire. The boarders and one or two other students from the university had gathered around her husband once again to hear his wise words and witty repartee. Catherine looked on at these young men as they bombarded her husband with question after question. She liked to listen in on their conversations, but was slightly concerned at the amount of notes they took.

In a lull in the conversation, which didn't happen that often, she whispered to Martin, 'Have you noticed how busy they are with their pens after dinner? They sneak quills and parchment up their sleeves and when you speak they are constantly scratching down almost everything you say – even your jokes!'

Martin grinned. He didn't seem to mind at all. The hour after dinner was one of the best hours of the day. Anyone could pop in to spend some time around the Luthers' fireside. The older children would find cosy corners by the hearth and listen – in much the same way Martin had done when he had been a young lad in Mansfeld. His father had deliberately invited intelligent men to their home, in order for Martin to listen and learn from the conversation.

'Don't worry, Katie,' he smiled at his loving wife. 'In a moment, I will take out my lute and we'll begin some music making.' This was another Luther family tradition, in which the children would sing sweetly, and anyone in the house who had an instrument to hand, would join in.

A feeble knock was heard at the door, to which both Martin and his wife turned round.

'I shall see who it is,' Catherine replied.

'If it is a beggar, let him into the warmth. We have supper left over, though no coin, I'm afraid; not tonight.'

Catherine sighed as she went to see what waif or stray needed their help. Nobody, if it could be helped, was ever turned away from the Luther family's door. Martin always spared whatever he could for a wandering student or homeless monk or beggar.

As his wife ushered a rather cold and sorrowful-looking old monk into the kitchen for some food, Martin stoked the fire again and thanked God for the blessing of a good wife.

'We are not wealthy, though she comes from an aristocratic background. Catherine had no money when she left the convent. Her family has nothing to do with her. But she is astute with money, capable and bright.' Thinking of the recent repairs made to their home, Martin knew that none of this would have been possible without Catherine.

Her work in the garden meant that it not only fed their family, but also provided extra income. She kept pigs and poultry, and the fruit trees that she had planted in previous years would eventually grow into impressive specimens. They even had a well-stocked fish pond. Catherine would be up in the early hours to milk cows and to see to the other farm animals. Martin particularly enjoyed the beer that she brewed. Brewing was an important skill for a housewife in the 1500s, when clean water wasn't always to be relied on.

Often, Catherine would take her husband aside and give him stern advice about the family finances. It was fine to give aid to those in genuine need, but she had often noted that many of the beggars that made their way to the Luther household were simply taking advantage of Martin's well-known soft heart.

Martin smiled warmly again as his wife returned from the kitchen, ushering the elderly monk to a warm spot by the fire.

He thought to himself, 'Next to God's Word, the world has no more precious treasure than holy matrimony. God's best gift is a pious, cheerful, god-fearing wife, with whom you may live peacefully, to whom you may entrust your goods, your body and life. Frau Cotta was right all those years ago. I should have listened to her. I should have listened to a great many good pieces of advice, but didn't. I know I can trust my Katie.'

And Martin did just that with Catherine. He needed to. Close friends and contacts recognised that without this woman, Martin would be leading a far poorer life. 'If left to himself, he would be a miserable, poor, flea-bitten bachelor,' someone remarked.

As it was, Martin was well looked after by his wife, as she cared for his daily needs and looked to ease the ailments and pain that he often suffered.

Throughout their marriage, Martin continued to debate with other theologians and, of course, he continued to write. It was Catherine's hard work and good sense that was the root of all this.

Writing had been a passion of his for a long time. In the year of his marriage, 1525, his book, *On the Bondage of the Will* was published. It was a response to a book previously published by the theologian Erasmus, which had appeared the previous year. The debate between the two men focused on the issue of whether after mankind fell into sin in the Garden of Eden – was humanity then free to choose between good and evil?

Luther argued that human beings were unable to bring themselves to God. Everything in the human nature, the human mind, soul and will, have been infected by the influence of sin. No one can be saved by their own choices. It is only by God changing the human heart that the individual attains salvation. The fact that God is all powerful supported Luther's position on this matter. To argue otherwise, Luther insisted, was an insult to God himself. In later years, Luther would look back on this particular book as one of his most important pieces of writing, one that he could really call his and his alone.

And with Catherine's help, the writing continued. In 1529, he wrote *The Great Catechism*, a manual for pastors and teachers, and *The Small Catechism*, which was written for the people themselves to memorise. And then in the early years of his marriage, he and others continued to work on the translation of the Old Testament.

A German translation of the Old Testament was eventually published in 1534. Again, he used day-to-day German language, something that would make the Bible accessible to the ordinary German citizen, so that the people could read it without hindrance.

The 1534 Bible became a popular and influential Bible translation. It had notes and prefaces added by Luther and woodcut images by Lucas Cranach, an important artist and designer who lived in Wittenberg, court painter to the electors of Saxony.

And then Luther wrote a prolific number of hymns. Sometime between the years of 1527 and 1529, he wrote what is arguably today his most famous hymn, also known as the Battle Hymn of the Reformation: *A Mighty Fortress is Our God*, based on Psalm 46. But as well as writing the words, he also composed the music. Luther loved music and saw how combining truth with music was a way of reaching out to all classes of people and all ages.

So that is why, as Catherine sat the elderly monk down beside his host in front of the fire, Luther took out his lute and gently began to sing, 'Ein feste Burg ist unser Gott'. It wasn't long before his children, his wife and even the old monk were either singing in harmony or humming along to the tune.

Martin loved to spend time with his children. Listening to their talk and endless questions was a pleasure, not a chore. One morning, all the Luther youngsters were in the garden with their father.

A puzzled voice piped up, 'Father, what is that bird we are hearing just now?' Young Magdalena tugged at her father's sleeve. She was sitting with him underneath the pear tree, as her other siblings were tending a vegetable plot at the far end of the garden. Luther smiled at her curious young face before replying, 'It is a nightingale, I believe, Lenchen,' using her family nickname.

'But those frogs are too noisy!' she complained.

Martin nodded. The girl, who had placed her slate and chalk on the ground to try and listen to the bird, was a bright little creature herself, one that had a particular warm spot in his heart. During one of his lamented journeys away from his home, his wife Catherine had realised how homesick he was. So she had asked Lucas Cranach, the court painter, to paint their young daughter, then a year old. The picture was then sent on to her father, who was at that time in Coburg. He had kept this picture close by, throughout his stay there.

'What a time that was,' Martin remembered. His father had died and he had been unable to visit his widowed mother. Luther had been again thrust into disagreements with the emperor. It had seemed a terrible time to him, separated from family, home and students.

He had indeed been overjoyed to finally return to Wittenberg.

'Let the wife make her husband glad to come home and let him make her sorry to see him leave.'

Martin smiled as he remembered the first time he came up with those words, and how so often he'd seen the truth of them as he had left from and returned to the family home.

As he listened to the bird and the noisy frogs, he pulled Lenchen closer. As he often did, he had thought of a lesson of faith there and then with his child by his side. He told his young daughter to listen. 'The bird is like our Lord Jesus. He is the nightingale, singing the song of the gospel. The frogs, now – they are like the heretics and false prophets trying to prevent us from hearing the wonderful Good News. My darling, think on those things, think on our Lord Jesus …'

'Yes,' Lenchen lisped, as there was a large missing tooth in the middle of her mouth. 'Our wonderful Lord Jesus.'

And Martin smiled. He delighted in all his children, but he had a special fondness in his heart for Lenchen, who had come so soon after the death of another much-loved child, Elizabeth. She had died before she had reached eight months old. He was glad that his parents had been at her christening, for it was only four years after that when his father had died and a year after that his mother had passed away also. The year after the infant's death had been a difficult one. That pain had caused Martin and Catherine to cling to the love and faithfulness of their God. With the heartache and Martin's increased pain and sickness, it had been an exhausting year. But the pain had not stopped Martin from his duty and passion of preaching the Word. Between Elizabeth's death and Magdalena's birth, Martin preached 200 times, in addition to taking household devotions every Sunday afternoon.

Family devotions were important to him. Teaching their children was a vital part of life for Martin and Catherine. It wasn't just the boys' education that mattered to them. Playfully pulling on Lenchen's pigtail, he could not help but feel a tender tug on his heart towards her and his other little girl, Margarete. It was not so easy for girls as it was for boys, he felt. This world was a cruel and harsh place for the young maiden who was uncared for and unprovided for. Martin could see how vulnerable they were in his society. 'Boys can do well if they get a job and work hard. Girls, on the other hand, do not have the same opportunities, so they must be cared for and protected.'

And one practical way that Martin cared for all the girls in Wittenberg was how he made sure that it was not just boys who would learn to read. As part of the Reformation, schools were being made for both boys and girls, which reminded him: he wanted to teach the children that hymn he had written, the first verse at least.

'Come, Lenchen, let's get the other children and we will sing together.'

'What will we sing today?' Lenchen asked, as she picked up her slate.

'I think we shall try:

From heaven above to earth I come,
To bear good news to every home;
Glad tidings of great joy I bring
Whereof I now will say and sing.'[2]

---

2. *Von Himmel hoch, da komm ich her.* Words: Martin Luther 1531.

And soon Hans, Martin, Paul and the youngest, Margarete, were all running from the far end of the garden towards the house. Luther was taking out his lute and soon the family was enjoying a time of musical praise together.

Martin exclaimed as they sang the last note of the hymn,

'Next to the Word of God, the noble art of music is the greatest treasure in the world.'

Lenchen pointed out, 'Father, I thought you said that was holy matrimony?'

Catherine, her mother, laughed and added, 'And so he did!'

Luther smiled at them both; there were two smart women in his family, keeping him right.

But the year 1542 saw the bright light that was Lenchen extinguished from this life. A serious sickness came on the thirteen-year-old girl. It was evident that she would not have long to live.

Seeing their child in such pain and suffering broke her parents' hearts. As they tried to comfort her, they both leant on the Lord Jesus for help, encouraging their young daughter to do the same.

In the end, her death was peaceful. As her father knelt at her bedside, he asked his daughter, 'Lenchen, my little daughter, you would like to stay with your father, but are you content to go to your Heavenly Father?'

To which Lenchen replied, 'Yes, dearest Father; as God wills.'

It wasn't long before she gave her last breath and Luther was left holding his young child in his arms, weeping and casting his cares on the Lord God.

'My daughter is now provided for in body and in soul. As Christians, we are more certain of eternal life than of anything else; for God, who has promised it to us for his dear Son's sake, cannot lie.'

The Lord God and his Word comforted Martin through fear, through sickness and through this last great sorrow – death.

Perhaps one of his other sorrows was his regret that the Reformation had not accomplished what he had really hoped for ... a reformation. Instead, there was a division between the Roman Catholic Church and what was now the Protestant Church. And then there were even divisions within that, as reformers disagreed with each other about what certain verses of Scripture really meant.

One of those disagreements was on what actually took place at the Lord's Supper. Was the bread and the wine the actual flesh and blood of the Lord Jesus? Luther thought it was, others like the reformer, Ulrich Zwingli, did not. However, there was a great desire amongst the leaders of the Reformation for unity. Pastors from South Germany pleaded with Luther for an opportunity to discuss the theological situation. Because Luther was too ill to travel, the delegates had to come to Wittenberg for the discussion. They had to agree to disagree. And even though the point over which they disagreed was the Lord's Supper, before the South Germans left Wittenberg, they all took communion together. Though they sadly disagreed, they still worshipped together and gave thanks for their Saviour's death and resurrection.

From this point on, Luther's health continuously deteriorated. However, it did not stop him from making a journey to the town of his birth. He had never had much to do with Eisleben since his parents had left it for the more profitable area of Mansfeld, but this time, he was returning in order to oversee a property dispute. Luther was respected by many and seen as a just and righteous man, one that could be trusted in difficult situations like this. His experience of the law would also have been beneficial. So despite his loving Catherine's entreaties, Luther left Wittenberg with two of his sons, Martin and Paul, being careful to write his wife frequently on the journey, telling her each time exactly what he had eaten that day.

On the 14th of February, 1546, he wrote a letter, 'To my dear, kind housewife, Catherine Luther von Bora,' and ended it with the acclamation, 'I have no ailments.' Perhaps this was wishful thinking.

However, he was never to see Catherine again. On the same day that he wrote that letter, he preached at the Church of St. Andrew with great enthusiasm, but had to cease preaching due to a sudden turn of weakness.

On the 17th of February, Martin underwent great suffering. It became steadily obvious that the reformer did not have long to live. Lying on his bed, he groaned in pain. As his life began to wither, someone knelt down beside him to ask, 'Do you stand by Christ and the doctrine that you have preached?'

Luther opened his eyes just a little, to reply, 'Yes.' That was his last word.

On the 18th of February he died, barely 100 yards away from the building in which he had taken his first breath, over sixty years previously. It was an unusual end to this fiery, reforming life. He had gone full circles from peasant to priest and back again, to the very spot where his parents had begun a dream of better things for their son. The truth was, God had better plans than their dreams – better plans for a country, a church and the world.

They laid him to rest in the Castle Church of Wittenberg, near to the door where he had nailed his Theses, where the fire of the Reformation first started.

Martin Luther:
Timeline

1483	Birth of Martin Luther in Germany.
1484	Hans and Margarethe Luther move their family to Mansfeld.
1497	Luther goes to school in Mansfeld and then Magdeburg.
1498	Luther goes to school in Eisenach.
1501	Luther goes to the University of Erfurt.
1505	Luther receives his Master's degree and enters the Augustinian cloister on 17th July, 1505.
1507	Luther is ordained as a priest.
1508	Staupitz sends for Luther to teach theology at Wittenberg.
1512	Luther is awarded his Doctorate in Theology.
1516	John Tetzel sent to Germany by the Roman Catholic Church to sell indulgences.
	Luther is made superintendent of eleven Augustinian convents.
1517	'95 Theses' nailed to the door of the Castle Church in Wittenberg.
1518	Luther meets the papal legate at Augsburg.
	Luther attends the General Assembly at Heidelberg.
1519	By this date, Luther's Theses had been translated into French, English and Italian and he had published a commentary on Galatians and the Psalms.

1520	Leipzig Disputation.
	Luther publishes: *To the Christian Nobility of the German Nation; On the Babylonian Captivity of the Church; On the Freedom of a Christian.*
1521	Diet of Worms; Charles V proclaims a ban on Luther, declaring that he could be legally killed.
1521	Luther finds refuge at the castle called Wartburg.
1522	Luther secretly returns to Wittenberg.
	Luther translates New Testament into German.
1525	Luther publishes *On the Bondage of the Will,* in response to Erasmus.
	Luther marries Catherine von Bora.
1526	Luther's first child, Hans, is born.
1527	Elizabeth, Luther's first daughter, is born.
1528	Elizabeth, Luther's first born daughter, dies.
1529	Magdalena, Luther's second daughter, is born.
1531	Luther's second son, Martin, is born.
1533	Luther's third son, Paul, is born.
1534	Margarete, Luther's youngest daughter, is born.
	Old and New Testaments now published in German.
1542	Magdalena, Luther's second daughter, dies aged thirteen.
1546	Martin Luther dies.

Fact Files

Germany

Today, we know Germany as a united nation. However, in the year 1356, there were seven rulers in Germany, called prince-electors who were answerable to the Emperor Charles IV, Emperor of the Holy Roman Empire. In the 18th Century, the Holy Roman Empire consisted of approximately 1,800 territories. After the fall of Napoleon, the German Confederation was founded as a loose league of thirty-nine sovereign states. In 1871, the German princes proclaimed the founding of the German Empire, uniting all German areas, except for Austria. At this point, Berlin became the nation's capital.

Holy Roman Empire

During the Early Middle Ages, there was a large complex of territories that spread across central Europe. It began on the 25th of December, 800, when Pope Leo III crowned Charlemagne as emperor. The term Holy Roman Empire was not used until the 13th Century, however. After the year 962, the largest part of the empire was the kingdom of Germany, although it also included the Kingdom of Bohemia, the Kingdom of Burgundy and the Kingdom of Italy, amongst other territories. The German prince electors, the highest ranking noblemen of the empire, usually elected one of their peers who would later be crowned emperor by the pope. The power of the emperor was limited as the various princes, lords, bishops and cities of the empire were, on the whole, independent, although they owed the emperor their allegiance. The Holy Roman Empire was dissolved in 1806.

Jewish Controversy

After reading this book, you will know that Luther caused controversy. His life was full of it. Some of the controversy he caused was essential, in order for the church to reform. He had to shake the church up. He had to make people take a long, hard look at their lives, their beliefs, their actions. But even today, people are still arguing about the things he said. Some of what he said was wrong. For example, he spoke against the Jewish people and said things like, 'The Jews are the most miserable people on earth.' But it's important to point out that Luther also spoke out fiercely against the German people when he felt the need to. He could speak with a sharp tongue. But he loved the Lord Jesus, the Word of God – and longed for all sinners to come to Christ, Jews included. It was perhaps his frustration that so few Jewish people were converted, that caused him to speak out against them so harshly.

It is a fact that he was human, and with humanity comes sin and failure. Luther had his own fair share of that – as do we all. He made mistakes in the religious sphere and in the political. He gave good advice to some and bad advice to others. And often a lot of what he said was written down without his consent. How many of us would like to have all our jokes and tweets gathered together and published? It is important to realise that some of what Luther said was said in jest, and some of what he said he may have wished unsaid at a later date.

The Peasants' War

This was a widespread popular revolt in the German-speaking areas of central Europe between the years 1524 and 1525. The conflict was the largest and most widespread prior to the French Revolution of 1789. Between 100,000 and 300,000 peasants and farmers were slaughtered by the ruling aristocracy. The revolt took some of its inspiration from the Reformation. The peasants sought freedom and influence, which was also sought by the reformers. Martin Luther criticised the injustice imposed on the peasants and he criticised the peasants for fighting back. He could not support the peasants because they were breaking the peace, and he could not support the ruling classes because they showed no mercy and suppressed the people cruelly. Many have criticized Luther for the position he took. However, it must have been very difficult to take any position at this confusing time.

The Lord's Supper

Christians remember Christ's death and resurrection by celebrating The Lord's Supper. Roman Catholics and Lutherans refer to this as the Mass. The Roman Catholic Church believes that the bread and the wine become the body and blood of the Lord Jesus Christ during the Mass while only keeping an appearance of bread and wine.

During the Protestant Reformation this doctrine referred to as Transubstantiation became controversial. Martin Luther believed that Jesus Christ was still bodily present but only temporarily. The Roman Catholic Church believe that the bread and wine once they become the body and blood of Christ remain as that. Luther also disagreed with the Roman Catholic Church when they said that celebrating the mass was an act through which a sinner obtained salvation.

Not all the reformers agreed about what took place at the Lord's Supper. Reformers like Zwingli disagreed with Luther and believed that the bread and wine are symbols to represent Christ's body and blood based on the scripture: Luke 22:19. Reformed churches believe that Christ is present at the Lord's Supper in a spiritual sense.

Ecclesiastical Titles and Positions

The pope is the leader of the worldwide Roman Catholic Church. There is a hierarchy within the Roman Catholic church and cardinals are second in this hierarchy after the pope. They are appointed by the pope and on the death of a pope elect his successor. The other positions held in the Roman Catholic Church are as follows: archbishops, bishops and priests. A priest is a member of the clergy who has authority to administer the sacraments in the Roman Catholic Church. The bishop is a senior member of the clergy who oversees the priests. An archbishop is a bishop of the highest rank who has authority over a particular area and all the church matters that arise within that.

Within convents and monasteries there are also different positions one mentioned throughout this book is prior. The word prior comes from the Latin for earlier or first. It is an ecclesiastical title for a superior person within the monastery who is lower in rank than an abbot. The female equivalent is a prioress whose superior would be an abbess.

Thinking Further Topics

Chapters

1. Martin was afraid of the thunder and lightning. He knew he had to pray. But what mistakes did he make about prayer? Read: Matthew chapter 6. How does Jesus tell us to pray?

2. Martin's parents wanted a good education for him. But what is the most important thing in life? Read: 1 Corinthians 10:31; Psalm 73:24-26 and John 17:22; 24.

3. What was wrong about the picture Martin saw in Magdeburg? How do we really get to heaven? Look up 2 Timothy 1:8-9; Ezekiel 11:19; John 6:44-45; Philippians 2:13; Ephesians 3:5.

4. Martin prayed to dead saints. This is not what the Bible tells us to do. What do you think prayer is? Look up Psalm 62:8; Psalm 10:17; 1 John 5:14; John 16:23; Philippians 4:6.

5. Martin was taught the Ten Commandments. One commandment is: honour your father and mother. The Bible teaches us how to behave with our parents and others. Look up Ephesians 5:21-22; Ephesians 5:1, 5, 9; Romans 13:1 and Romans 12:10. Why should we keep this command? Ephesians 6:1-3.

6. How did Romans 1:17 change Martin? What did he believe before this? When he studied Romans, he discovered justification. This is when God freely pardons all our sins and accepts us as righteous – because the righteousness of Jesus Christ has been laid on us and God has given us faith to believe in Christ. Read: Ephesians 1:7; 2 Corinthians 5:19, 21; Romans 5:17-19; Romans 5:1.

7. Martin believed that no man could achieve his own salvation. Do you sometimes think that you need to do something to get to heaven? Good works are good, as they show others how lovely God is – but they are not good enough for salvation. When we trust in Christ for salvation, we are given many good things such as an assurance of God's love, peace, joy, grace and perseverance. Read these verses: Romans 5:1-2, 5; Romans 14:17; Colossians 1:10-11; Ephesians 3:16-18; 1 Peter 1:5.

8. One of the things Martin said in his '95 Theses' was that a Christian who sees someone needy but looks past him and buys an indulgence instead, receives not the pope's remission but God's wrath. How is what Martin says here like the story that Jesus told in Luke chapter 10?

9. Martin would not turn away from what he believed. Do you find it hard to stick up for your beliefs? Do your beliefs follow the Word of God? Read: Luke 9:62. What does this verse tell us about giving up?

10. Martin made good use of the printing press. Can you think of other inventions that Christians have used

for the Kingdom of God? Are there new inventions today that we can use to spread God's Word? Read: 1 Corinthians 10:31. Consider different things you do throughout your week – and how you can give glory to God through them.

11. Martin Luther said at the Diet of Worms that he was 'bound by the Scriptures'. What does that mean, do you think? How important is God's Word to you? Read: Proverbs 30:5; Mark 7:13; Luke 4:4; 2 Timothy 3:16; John 5:39.

12. 'If only this one book would be in every language, in every hand and in the eyes, ears and hearts of all people!' Martin exclaimed. Visit the website of Wycliffe Bible Translators to find out how many languages still do not have the whole Bible. How does the Bible describe the Bible? Read: Hebrews 4:12; Jeremiah 23:29.

13. After Lenchen's death, Martin said that 'As Christians we are more certain of eternal life than of anything else; for God, who has promised it to us for his dear Son's sake, cannot lie.' What do you believe about heaven? Who do you believe Jesus Christ is? Here are some verses in the Bible you can read: John 17:3; Mark 10:29-31; John 3:16; Mark 1:1; John 20:31; Romans 8:39; 1 Timothy 2:5.

Bibliography

Hazlitt, William, (Translated and edited by) *Martin Luther's Tabletalk: Luther's Comments on Life, the Church and the Bible,* Christian Focus Publications, republished in 2003.

Lindsay, Thomas, *Martin Luther: The Man Who Started the Reformation*, Christian Focus Publications, 2008.

Merle D'Aubigne, J. H., (Translated from the French by H. White), T*he Life and Times of Martin Luther,* Moody Press, Chicago, 1978.

Nichols, Stephen J., (edited by), *Martin Luther's 95 Theses,* Presbyterian and Reformed; First edition (7 Nov. 2012).

Pettegree, Andrew, *Brand Luther: How an Unheralded Monk Turned his Small Town into a Center of Publishing, Made Himself the Most Famous Man in Europe—and Started the Protestant Reformation*, Penguin Press (27 Oct. 2015).

Sears, Barnas, D.D., *Life of Luther,* originally published in 1850 by ASSU Copyright © 2010 Attic Books.

Website:
http://www.desiringgod.org/messages/martin-luther-lessonsfrom-his-life-and-labor)

Some Luther Quotes

These quotes are all taken from *Martin Luther's Tabletalk: Luther's Comments on life, the Church and the Bible. ISBN: 978-1-85792-415-2*

'No greater mischief can happen to a Christian people, than to have God's Word taken from them, or falsified, so that they no longer have it pure and clear. God grant we and our descendants be not witnesses of such a calamity.'

'Like as in the world a child is an heir only because it is born to inherit, even so, faith only makes such to be God's children as are born of the Word, which is the womb wherein we are conceived, born, and nourished, as the prophet Isaiah says. Now, as through such a birth we become God's children, (wrought by God without our help or doing,) even so, we are also heirs, and being heirs, are freed from sin, death, and the devil, and shall inherit everlasting life.'

'Better it were that God should be angry with us, than that we be angry with God, for he can soon be at union with us again, because he is merciful; but when we are angry with him, then the case is not to be helped.'

'God delights in our temptations, and yet hates them; he delights in them when they drive us to prayer: he hates them when they drive us to despair.'

'There is but one God,' says St Paul, 'and one mediator between God and man; namely, the man Jesus Christ, who gave himself a ransom for all.' Therefore, let no man think to draw near unto God or obtain grace of him, without this mediator, high-priest, and advocate.

It follows that we cannot through out good works, honesty of life, virtues, deserts, sanctity, or through the works of the law, appease God's wrath, or obtain forgiveness of sins; and that all deserts of saints are quite rejected and condemned, so that through them no human creature can be justified before God. Moreover, we see how fierce God's anger is against sins, seeing that by none other sacrifice or offering could they be appeased and stilled, but by the precious blood of the Son of God.

When Jesus Christ utters a word, he opens his mouth so wide that it embraces all heaven and earth, even though that word be but in a whisper. The word of the emperor is powerful, but that of Jesus Christ governs the whole universe.'

A Christian must be well-armed, grounded, and furnished with sentences out of God's Word, that so he may stand and defend religion and himself against the devil, in case he should be asked to embrace another doctrine.

Upright Christians pray without ceasing; though they pray not always with their mouths, yet their hearts pray continually, sleeping and waking; for the sigh of a true Christian is a prayer.

'The Lord our God is a God of humble and perplexed hearts, who are in need, tribulation, and danger. If we were strong, we should be proud and haughty. God shows his power in our weakness; he will not quench the glimmering flax, neither will he break in pieces the bruised reed.'

The love towards our neighbour must be like the pure and chaste love between bride and bridegroom, where all faults are connived at and borne with, and only the virtues regarded.

Believest thou? Then thou wilt speak boldly. Speakest thou boldly? Then thou must suffer. Sufferest thou? Then thou shalt be comforted. For faith, the confession thereof, and the cross, follow one upon another.

The most acceptable service we can do and show unto God, and which alone he desires of us, is, that he be praised of us; but he is not praised, unless he be first loved; he is not loved, unless he be first bountiful and does well; he does well when he is gracious; gracious he is when he forgives sins. Now who are those that love him? They are that small flock of the faithful, who acknowledge such graces, and know that through Christ they have forgiveness of their sins. But the children of this world do not trouble themselves herewith.'

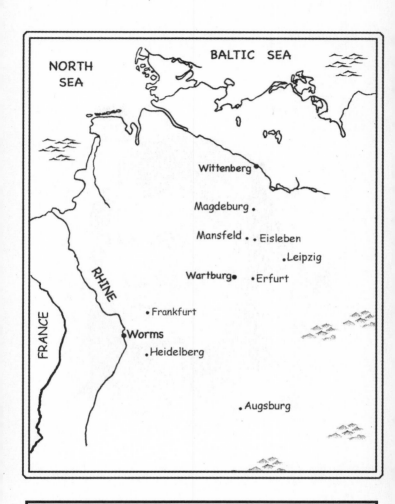

PART OF THE HOLY ROMAN EMPIRE AT THE TIME OF MARTIN LUTHER

Author Information

Catherine Mackenzie lives in the Highlands of Scotland and works as an author and children's editor. She has written over eighty titles. Several of these are youth biographies in the Trailblazer series such as:

Joni Eareckson Tada: Swimming Against the Tide
Richard Wurmbrand: A Voice in the Dark
John Calvin: After Darkness Light

Her books for younger children include the series: *Little Lights* – full colour biographies on well-known Christians.

Catherine has worked with children's ministries for several years through Sunday schools and youth camps. But she also has a perfect home-based audience of eight nieces and nephews.

TRAIL BLAZERS

• Ulrich Zwingli •

SHEPHERD WARRIOR

William Boekestein

Ulrich Zwingli: Shepherd Warrior
by William Boekestein

In a small Swiss village, nestled in the Alps, a young boy was born. The year of his birth was 1484. By the end of his brief life Ulrich Zwingli would change the religious landscape of his home and the world.

It wasn't until the last few years of his life that he became a reformer. He fought for truth and righteousness with his mind and pen, he fought for lost souls to hear the good news of Jesus Christ, and at the age of forty-seven, as an army chaplain, he was killed on the battle-field. Even to the last he continued his life's passion of caring for the souls of others. The Shepherd Warrior, Ulrich Zwingli, fought the good fight.

With his last strength he voiced his victory: 'They can kill the body but not the soul!'

ISBN: 978-1-78191-803-6

· John Calvin ·
AFTER DARKNESS LIGHT

Catherine Mackenzie

John Calvin: After Darkness Light
by Catherine Mackenzie

Calvin had ideas on how we could live better lives —
particularly how we could live in close harmony with
God and each other — but because his ideas were radical,
his life was filled with dramatic events and dangers. He
was run out of town — and then welcomed back. He
was accused of being too harsh — and also too tender
hearted. When he explained what the bible meant he
was considered too logical and too spiritual! He must
have been an amazing man to have caused such a stir!

ISBN: 978-1-78191-550-9

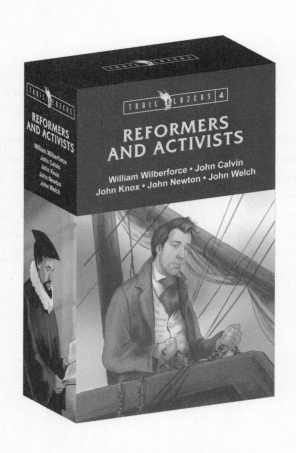

TRAIL BLAZERS 4

REFORMERS
AND ACTIVISTS

William Wilberforce • John Calvin
John Knox • John Newton • John Welch

Trailblazer Reformers and Activists Box Set 4

This giftbox collection of colourful trailblazer stories makes a perfect present that will delight young minds. Features some of the great Christian reformers and activists who will inspire young and old alike. This edition includes William Wilberforce, the man fought to bring freedom and relief from the terrors of the slave trade and John Knox, who went from being a bodyguard to a preacher of God's Word.

ISBN 978-1-78191-637-7

OTHER BOOKS IN THE TRAILBLAZERS SERIES

For a full list of Trailblazers, please see our website: www.christianfocus.com
All Trailblazers are available as e-books

Adventure and Faith
by Linda Finlayson

Martin Luther shakes in his boots. Accused of being a criminal and in danger of loosing his life he has to stand up for what he believes. **David Brainerd** ventures into difficult wilderness territory in order to share the gospel. There are tough decisions to make during his travels. The risks are great but so are the needs. **William King** simply obeys the Bible. It doesn't matter what the rich and powerful slave owners want – Jesus has other plans. **Brother Andrew** risks his life so that Hungarians can read the Bible. But what about the Soviet troops who have invaded the country? **Nehemiah** builds a wall while enemies plot to destroy his work. **Stephen** prays to Jesus as an angry mob throws stones at him. These men were all willing to take risks. They faced danger and difficulties. Some even died for what they believed in. While reading their exciting stories you will learn about why they did what they did and who it was who helped them.

ISBN: 978-1-84550-491-5